REFLECTIONS OF LIFE

From the Tree Stand and Trout Hole

Robert Shelton, DMin

WESTBOW
PRESS®
A DIVISION OF THOMAS NELSON
& ZONDERVAN

Scripture taken from the King James Version of the Bible.

Scripture taken from the Holy Bible, NEW INTERNATIONAL VERSION®. Copyright © 1973, 1978, 1984, 2011 by Biblica, Inc. All rights reserved worldwide. Used by permission. NEW INTERNATIONAL VERSION® and NIV® are registered trademarks of Biblica, Inc. Use of either trademark for the offering of goods or services requires the prior written consent of Biblica US, Inc.

Scripture quotations are from The Holy Bible, English Standard Version® (ESV®), copyright © 2001 by Crossway, a publishing ministry of Good News Publishers. Used by permission. All rights reserved.

This book is a work of non-fiction. Unless otherwise noted, the author and the publisher make no explicit guarantees as to the accuracy of the information contained in this book and in some cases, names of people and places have been altered to protect their privacy.

WestBow Press books may be ordered through booksellers or by contacting:

WestBow Press
A Division of Thomas Nelson & Zondervan
1663 Liberty Drive
Bloomington, IN 47403
www.westbowpress.com
1 (866) 928-1240

Because of the dynamic nature of the Internet, any web addresses or links contained in this book may have changed since publication and may no longer be valid. The views expressed in this work are solely those of the author and do not necessarily reflect the views of the publisher, and the publisher hereby disclaims any responsibility for them.

Any people depicted in stock imagery provided by Thinkstock are models, and such images are being used for illustrative purposes only. Certain stock imagery © Thinkstock.

ISBN: 978-1-5127-5166-6 (sc)
ISBN: 978-1-5127-5167-3 (e)

Library of Congress Control Number: 2016912312

Print information available on the last page.

WestBow Press rev. date: 09/13/2016

Dedicated to all the game wardens at the Arkansas Game and Fish Commission who keep us safe while preserving our natural heritage.

CONTENTS

INTRODUCTION

Words have power. They can encourage or discourage. They frame thoughts and forge ideas. Often they transport us to past memories or tomorrow's dreams. *Reflections of Life* journals the outdoor experience while looking for life's deeper meaning. Truth is only valuable if we apply it to our life. Learning from our failures builds character, so each outdoor experience creates chapters of life that produce wisdom.

There is a rhythm in God's creation. When we hit the trail, climb the tree, or fish a stream, we are applying for new wisdom to be added to the hard drive of our souls.

ACKNOWLEDGMENTS

To my wife, Jan, who has shared my passion for the outdoors for a lifetime. Her skill with grammar and sentence structure was a godsend.

And to Misty Sevenstar, who has labored with us for fifteen years. Her organization, ideas, and computer skills helped to make *Reflections of Life* a reality.

To my hunting and fishing friends who invested their time to teach me about life.

Finally, to Woodrow, whose unique philosophy of outdoor life has been a constant flow of life and laughter for me.

CHAPTER 1

Why Hunters Get Lost

I f you have been a hunter for any length of time, you have been lost. When Daniel Boone was asked if he had ever been lost in the woods, he replied, "No, but I have been a might turned around for three or four weeks." Most hunters, when lost, are less than a quarter of a mile from their destination.

Even with all of the gadgets like GPS, digital compasses, topo maps, and cell phone apps for every purpose under heaven, we still get lost. Even the glow-in-the-dark tacks can't seem to keep us from getting lost.

> *When Daniel Boone was asked if he had ever been lost in the woods, he replied, "No, but I have been a might turned around for three or four weeks."*

I love the adventure of scouting new woods. To see ground never covered before gives just a taste of how the mountain men must have felt as they engaged the Rocky Mountains. Boatmen who explored the great rivers and made maps for us while eagerly awaiting what was around the next bend of the river did us a great service. In their journals, they told of Native American tribes they encountered. They named creeks and tributaries so that we can know where we are today.

Great names like Bridger, Fitzpatrick, Carson, and Jedadiah Smith met mountain tribes, opened trading with them, and cleared a path for settlers. The Lewis and Clark expedition journals gave Americans an appetite "to see the elephant," as they would say. Those great adventurers were often lost for weeks while looking for a pass to get through the Rockies. That is the risk of seeking new ground. You may just get lost.

Being lost begins with a state of mind. As you begin to look for deer signs, you walk while looking down. This causes you to lose the peripheral perspective that you naturally have while looking forward. And the deeper the woods, the more desperate the feeling that you are lost. When fear sends a panic message to the brain, all the trees begin to look alike and all trails seem to spin you in a circle. Panic is the enemy of any outdoorsman. To panic is to give in to the fear that is now driving the mind. You begin to walk faster, as though that will give clear direction. The mind jumps to conclusions that it may be a long, cold night.

Losing cell phone service and having low GPS batteries brings panic. That is being lost. Being lost brings a fear that your pride might be wounded. No one ever wants to admit that they are lost, as that is the ultimate insult. That is also why we men never want to look at maps while traveling. We want to believe we always know where we are and where we are going.

Even worse is to be lost and not even know it. This fall, I drew in on a muzzleloader hunt with my son, Shawn, and my hunting buddy, Matt Brown. This special hunt was on the Black River in northeast Arkansas. The swamp and the cypress trees along with the winding river had me turned around from the moment I stepped onto the wildlife management area of twenty-seven thousand acres. Matt knew the area well, as he grew up hunting on the Black River, so he served as our guide.

On the second morning of the hunt, I decided to explore on my own. In the darkness of the early morning, I marked my position on the GPS. I walked off into unknown ground, followed a drainage creek, and came to an oak flat that opened up nicely. Along the creek, the swamp gave way to an oak flat that formed a small funnel that looked like deer would use, so I made some ground cover, concealed myself well, and got my muzzleloader ready to do its job. A nice eight-point came through the funnel, but I did not get a shot at him. Sometimes things just go south on you in the field. The buck never spooked; he just vanished. I marked the waypoint on my GPS. I was only a quarter of a mile from my truck. It was a short walk into the unknown to see such a nice buck. Within minutes, I heard whistling coming across the oak flat, which I thought unusual. The unseen man wanted to make sure I knew of his presence. The only guys who do that in the woods are the game wardens who patrol them, and in a moment I saw the warden move over to my area. We engaged in conversation. I produced my license and the special WMA permit. He asked if I had seen anything. I told him about the close call with the monster eight-point. He said, "Well, I am sorry that you didn't get him, and I'm even more sorry to tell you that you have wandered off the WMA and are on private land." My brain was shooting out messages like *Seriously? This is a 27,000-acre area, and I walked off of it on a hike that took only ten minutes?* I was taken aback. I didn't even realize I was lost. Officer David was very kind to me and demonstrated grace on my behalf.

Deer never seem to be lost. They are never looking for a waypoint because they have nothing to get back to. They can lie down where they want. They wander into a soybean field and then find good cover to rest without any thought of how to get back. They do not panic because they have no stuff to worry about. We get lost because of stuff. We are trying to make our way back to a truck that we own. We are lost because we are away from the home that we call ours—and must return to. All forest creatures will just make a new home for the night if need be. Humans are stuff huggers. We have to have stuff. We love going to hunting stores to buy more stuff to carry with us while we hunt. The animals operate efficiently in the wild because they don't get lost; they just move on to what's next for them without fear or panic that they may get lost.

There is a spiritual application of being lost that we must address. To be lost means that you do not have a personal relationship with Jesus Christ as your Savior. It brings a panic and desperation for peace that only the

3

love of Christ can bring to a heart. When we confess our sin to the Lord, we are acknowledging that we are lost. We are also admitting that we want to be found. The Good Shepherd finds us in our "lostness," and brings us to a new life in Him. Redemption comes where confession is made. Call upon Him ... He knows where you are.

All hunters have a secret desire to be a Jeremiah Johnson, or a Kit Carson, just as long as our pickup is a quarter of a mile from the road.

CHAPTER 2

Losing Light

(Waste Time ... Waste Life)

I am the light of the world; he that follows me shall not
walk in darkness, but shall have the light of life.
—John 8:12

When Christians make poor choices, they are usually in the dark. "Consider the fact that light traveling 186,000 miles per second only takes eight minutes to travel the 93 million miles between the Sun and planet earth."

This is a phrase in hunting that refers to the last possible second that a hunter can legally shoot at an animal. In most states, shooting is to stop a half hour before sundown. This of course is a good rule to prevent making bad shots with low light. Wounding an animal because of a bad shot rather than being able to harvest one is simply a poor choice.

When a hunter is in the magic evening zone and the world begins to still itself, anticipation mounts. Then a rifle shot is heard across the valley. *Why not me?* you think. There's still time. A nice buck just has to step out into the clearing. Then the struggle begins with the clock. Down to just minutes, looking through the scope to ensure there is enough light to make a safe shot is a constant. Suddenly, like a switch, the guardian of the woods turns the daylight off, the headlight goes on, and it's hike time back to the truck. Shooting light is lost.

When Christians make poor choices, they are usually in the dark. Consider the fact that light traveling 186,000 miles per second only takes eight minutes to travel the ninety-three million miles between the sun and planet earth; so the sunlight that warms your back and gives you shooting light for the hunt is only eight minutes old when you first see it. When light shines on us, there is no darkness. Light and darkness cannot coexist together. It's one thing for a child to be afraid of the dark, but quite another when a grown man runs from the light.

When the daylight gives way to the shadows of darkness, you lose shooting light. In life, each day is divided into day and night. This is how we measure time. "So teach us to number our days that we may apply our hearts unto wisdom." Psalm 90:12 (KJV) While time is measured in minutes, life is measured in moments. So remember to savor each moment, for soon, shooting light will be lost. The older I get, the more I detest wasting time. When I waste time, I waste life. We are not in control of our life spans. We are, however, in charge of our lives' significance. We are bound by time. Just as we lose shooting light, we lose living light. Jesus reminded us of this truth in John 9:4 (KJV) "I must work the works of him that sent me, while it is day: the night cometh, when no man can work."

The Bible tells us in 1 John 1:7 (KJV) to "walk in the light." It is sure easier when we do. Light creates security. For the child afraid of the dark, keeping the light on allows them to go to sleep without fear. For the hunter making his way out of the woods, a bright light makes them feel confident that all is well. While I am not afraid to be alone in the woods after dark, I am a light freak. I actually carry two backup flashlights in my pack. What hunter has not forgotten their flashlight or had the batteries run down while trying to make it through the woods? It's tough walking in the dark. We trip, fall, and bump into trees and walk into giant spider webs. Darkness does that. Once I was called upon to visit a man on suicide watch in a facility. When I entered his room, it was void of any light. There were no windows in the room. He was sitting in a chair and peering out into darkness. It was an eerie feeling. I asked if I could please turn the light on, and he refused. He said, "I am used to the darkness." That statement haunted me for a long time. Why would anyone want to get used to the darkness? We need light. The body requires it, and the soul demands it. Depression is a close cousin of darkness. Our moods are deeply affected by the absence of light.

There is just nothing like sitting in a tree stand and watching that giant yellow ball as it makes its entrance into the day. I love those moments in the stand when we have to just sit and wait for the light. Without it, there can be no hunting. Without it, you will make poor choices and stumbling will be a constant in your life.

When we turn the lights off each night, there is an expectation that tomorrow there will be light. Don't come to the end of your life with deep regrets that you wasted time, which wasted life.

CHAPTER 3

Focus

The Hunter's Edge

I sat down on a log under an oak tree to rest and get my bearings. The forest had such life in them. The gold and red hues of the trees captured my attention. Acorns were falling like small bombs everywhere as I followed a small drainage creek to a comfortable log. My goal was to scout the new ground while stalking. Watching two gray squirrels chase each other, I realized that I was seeing the last days of fall. Soon, the trees would be bare and the long winter would begin. I was brought back to reality when my cell phone vibrated four times. *Oh no, I* thought. *It must be the church and something is wrong.*

I grabbed the phone from my pocket and began reading the texts. I fired back an answer and hit send. Just as I did, I realized I was being watched, not by two squirrels but by a buck that was either an eight or ten point. He was about twenty-five yards away. He stood erect and lifted up his huge neck. An attempt to move any part of my body would not go well. Our standoff lasted

> *I learned a great lesson about hunting and life that morning. A good hunter tries to eliminate distractions, but a great hunter has FOCUS.*

about thirty seconds. He never blew or stomped his feet at me. He turned broadside and I thought, *Here is my chance.* I eased the phone down on the log beside me and the buck said adios. No white flag. He just turned and walked away. As he did, he turned back and looked at me one last time as if to say, "That was strange."

I learned a great lesson about hunting and life that morning. A good hunter tries to eliminate distractions, but a great hunter has *focus*. It is difficult to leave the world and its worries behind, but consider why you go to all the trouble and expense to be a hunter. Is it so that you can answer texts from the stand? Do you want to be able to catch the 5:00 news while scouting a new area? No, you want to escape. You want to explore without thinking about the pressures of life. In order to achieve focus, you must be intentional. There are many hunting gadgets that you place in your backpack that actually distract you. Your natural senses are honed when you pressure them to become better. Sight, hearing, taste, smell, and touch can do more to help you focus on your purpose of becoming a great hunter than everything else.

You can purchase expensive sound enhancement, but absolutely no gadget can match the miracles on each side of your head. It is possible to walk past fresh rubs and scrapes without noticing them because you are not focused. The first time I ever smelled an elk wallow, I almost gagged, but paying attention to that smell can help you find the big bulls. Sitting in a tree stand fiddling with a phone is a good way to be a bad hunter.

David said, "For I am fearfully and wonderfully made." Psalm 139:14 (KJV) God created us for His glory and in His image. Take those natural senses into the woods and focus. You will become a much better hunter. The same is true of the nonhunting world of family, faith, and finances. Focus as much on your family as you do your hunting. Focus on your purpose in life. It takes work. It requires time and passion. Finding balance in life will always be demanding.

When we are running from decisions that we need to make or avoiding conflict at home, don't make hunting your alibi. Engage the issues before you seek escape. We all tend to dodge dealing with situations that we don't want to think about. When there seems to be no answer for your problems, you lose focus. Learn to become solution orientated with life issues. If you run from them, they only grow. If you continue to bury the problem rather than deal with it, you lose focus. I hate to leave a problem without closure. It is better to just call a time-out and deal with critical issues now. Make your apologies if needed, right the wrong if possible, concede the moral high ground if necessary, but begin now.

Many years ago, I had an unresolved conflict. I cannot even remember what it was. But I do remember taking no action. I also remember thinking, *Forget it*! I grabbed my golf clubs and went to the golf course. I paid my green fee and rented a walking cart. My anger was present in every swing. I am glad I was playing alone. By the third hole, I was steaming. Golf and anger are not good traveling companions. I wised up and walked back to the club house rather than going to the fourth hole. I put the clubs away and jumped into handling the thing I should have handled before I ran away to the golf course.

Focus is paramount in all areas of life. Texting and driving? Bad. Golfing and angry? Very bad. Hunting after screaming at your wife and children? Forget it. "To everything, there is a season." Learn to focus on what is in front of you. Handle bad stuff when it is in front of you. Enjoy the good times of life as they happen naturally. The Lord gave us the perfect tree stand verse. "Be still ... and know that I am God." Psalm 46:10 (KJV)

CHAPTER 4

Hangin' in the Harness

(Prepping for the Future)

Watch therefore: for you know not what
hour your Lord doth come.
—Matthew 24:42

O n a cold central Missouri afternoon, nestled between two cornfields in a narrow strip of hardwoods, my day came to an abrupt stop. The heavy north winds had made the afternoon hunt difficult. In my anticipation of getting to my stand, I had made a horrible mistake. After my son dropped me off by the cornfield, I realized I had forgotten my safety harness. Knowing that, I carefully climbed the tree and sat as still as possible. Eventually the strong winds, however, dictated I get to safety. Climbing down, I decided to take the stand with me. This was normally my son's job. Shawn was hunting about five miles away on a farm, so I thought I would do the deed. Big mistake! While on the top step of the ladder, I released the wrong ratchet, instantly causing the stand to collapse.

Several minutes later, I woke up. My right knee was hyperextended under me, and I could not get my breath. After lying there a while, I struggled to my feet and could walk. I took the stand off the tree and started through the cornfield. Shawn had dropped me off and was to pick me up after shooting light by the farm road. I had no cell service, and it was only 2:30 in the afternoon. I lay down in the high grass, hoping the farmer who lived about a mile away might come down the road and take me to the other farm where Shawn was hunting. Not realizing that I was in shock, I fell asleep. When I woke up, it was dark and cold. Finally, I saw the lights of a truck. It was Shawn. We got to the little motel and crashed for the night. The mistake of not prepping for the unknown could have cost me my life. A cracked sternum and torn muscles in the knee were the price I paid for a terrible mistake.

The reason I wanted to take the stand down myself was that Shawn had fallen the day before, injuring his ankle while hanging his stand. I taped him with duct tape not, realizing that he had broken his ankle. His condition was more serious than we thought. He suffered greatly and spent two months in a hard cast.

This trip is referred to by our family as "the hunting trip from Hades." We also had three flats on my truck during the hunting trip. As we left the motel, we had to help each other get in the truck. We looked at each other and burst into laughter at our pitiful condition. What a trip!

While we might be commended for our "never quit" spirit, we are both smarter than that. To prep for the unknown is a must each time we step into the field or forest. Now my routine before any hunt always includes my safety procedures. Carrying weapons that can kill us is enough reason to think safety first. Add to that climbing twenty feet in the air while hanging onto a tree, which is more than enough reason to prep for the unknown.

> *Bad habits are hard to break and good habits are hard to keep.*

There is a parallel between prepping for the hunt and for life. As Christians we are told to be diligent and serious about life and the decisions that we make. When we are careless about things, their value is diminished. When we suffer from our carelessness, it is a huge wake-up call. Now, safety is a habit. No one has to remind me.

Smart people make dumb decisions every day. When we do, there is always a price to pay. There is always a consequence to our actions. Bad habits are hard to break, and good habits are hard to keep. To do the right thing is a habit. To prepare for what could happen is just plain smart.

CHAPTER 5

The Science of Not Freaking Out

(Finding Emotional Balance)

He who is slow to anger is better than the mighty, and
he who rules his spirit, than he who captures a city.
—Proverbs 16:32

Keeping our emotions under control can be a real challenge while hunting and in nonhunting activities that require breathing. I have heard of people who hyperventilate because a buck steps out in front them. I have witnessed people throwing up because they were so excited during the intense moment of making a shot. Keeping emotions in check, whether as a spectator at a ball game or as a hunter stalking your prey, is a full-time job.

Anxiety is an American staple. We worry about everything. Our anxiety has led us to become the most over medicated generation in history.

When we get a case of the nerves, Paul's advice from Philippians 4:6 is always good. "Be anxious for nothing, but in everything by prayer and supplication with thanksgiving let your request be made known to God."

Anxiety is an American staple. We worry about everything. Our anxiety has led us to become the most overmedicated generation in history.

Hunters cannot find peace and balance for life if they are constantly worried about that life. If you miss a twenty-yard bow shot, no amount of stomping, cursing, or throwing things from your stand will give you another opportunity to do that shot. It's over. Learn from your mistake and don't freak out. You are not guaranteed a kill just because you went to all the effort to go hunting. Opportunity is all you get, and even those don't happen all the time.

Hunting is a reflection of your life. If you are anxious and fretful about life, you will be the same dressed in camo. If you take pleasure only in killing something, you are not a hunter; you are psychotic. You must learn to find fulfillment in the process itself. Everything in life is about expectation. Tell a child that you are taking him or her for a big surprise in three days, and the next seventy-two hours might just be the longest that you ever spend. Why? Because you created expectation, and expectation creates anxiety. Now the child must deal with patience while you deal with impatience. You must learn that anticipation is a God-given emotion not to make you sick but to make you thankful. Anticipation can be more rewarding than the actual event.

You will never become a good hunter until you can control your emotions. If you are anxious, easy shots can be missed. Aiming and shaking are not good partners. A great hunter showed me a trick once. He learned to breathe through a straw when he was nervous. No matter how anxious, he kept breathing slowly through the straw. It reinforced in him the habit of keeping his mouth closed during tense moments. It also regulated his breathing.

The Chris Kyle story is unique. We have learned much about the mind of a person who is called to do a horrible job. The military sniper is trained in keeping their heart rate down during unsettling moments. They don't react to things going wrong. They do, however, execute their training without flaw, regardless of what is happening around them.

Stress is something we work hard to avoid. That is a mistake. It is the stress itself that teaches you how to respond to things going wrong. Jesus asked three men to sit up with Him one night and just keep watch so that He could pray. His soul was physically stressed because the cross was awaiting Him. The three men He chose did not have that data. Therefore, they all went to sleep. They had no stress and were not anxious. Jesus called a time-out during His ordeal and talked to the Father. That should be our action as well. Peter, James, and John would live long enough to suffer many lonely nights in agony just like the Savior had done in the Garden of Gethsemane. Stress depletes the body's strength and can rob us of joy. There will always be stress, but it does not have to turn into anxiety. When Jesus came back the third time and saw the disciples asleep again, in Matthew 26:45 (KJV) He said, "Sleep on now." He had made peace with the problem. That should be our goal when stressed. Work through it, make peace with the problem, and move on.

American hunters are blessed. It is one of the few nations left on earth that we can put a rifle or a bow in our vehicle and head to the woods. We do, however, have to obey the laws, we have to practice a consideration for others, and we have to keep our emotions in check.

I do not believe everyone should carry a gun. I didn't say they should not have a right to. I am a Second Amendment person to the core of my being. People who cannot control their emotions also cannot control the weapon they hold in their hands. We do not need more gun laws passed. We need people who recognize the awesome responsibility of owning a gun. The man who shot and killed American hero Chris Kyle could not control his emotions and therefore could not control anything else in his life.

Our government officials believe they have the answer: just take all guns away from all people. Seems like they tried that in Chicago already. Hunting is not for everybody, and I am uncomfortable to see young boys or girls in deer stands with guns that cannot control their emotions. Angry boys with guns have almost destroyed the freedom we hold dear. Train your children not to react every time something happens to them. If they are allowed to react with a negative outburst, they do not need to be in the field with a weapon. If parents would take time for teaching moments to deal with the unchecked emotions of their child at home, then the hunting experience can be a positive reinforcement of that training. There is not enough training about guns and handling them. Our concealed weapon training, while good, is not nearly enough. It should be at least a twenty-hour block of instruction. This is serious stuff. This is also why many Americans look at hunters as a bunch of redneck hillbillies who ride in the back of pickup trucks and kill animals while carrying large spotlights.

You should not be a hunter just because you have camo or because you have a right to be. You should be a hunter because you accept the overwhelming responsibility to be a person who demonstrates character from twenty feet up in the air or with feet firmly on the ground.

CHAPTER 6

The Unspoken Law

(Ethics and the Hunter)

Better is a poor man who walks in his integrity,
than he who is perverse in speech and is a fool.
—Proverbs 19:1

We are challenged by it all the time. Ethics. It is defined as "moral principles that govern a person's or group's behavior." It is also seen as values, a moral code, or a standard that we hold as dear. This philosophy deals with morality. What does that have to do with the outdoors? Practically everything. Who we are is a result of what we do. That is ethics.

As sportsmen and women who revere the outdoors, this ethic or moral code must play a large part in our decision making. Once while hanging stands in Missouri, we were faced with just such a moral dilemma. It was the night before the gun season began. My son Shawn got a lock-on stand in place, centered beside a large cornfield and a nice cover of oaks. He was testing out the stand with about a half hour of daylight left. Out of nowhere, a nice buck jumped the fence and eased over to hide in the cover of the hardwoods. It was an easy shot. He had a clear shooting lane.

The buck was in his sights. He whispered down to me that it was a heavy eight point.

The moral dilemma was that the season would not start until the following morning at shooting light. No, he did not shoot. The buck lived to enjoy another day. A moral dilemma begins in our mind when faced with right and wrong. All hunters must make up their minds that there are things that are right and things that are wrong. When hunters drive along country roads after dark with the intent to spotlight a deer, they have no ethic. They are not sportsmen. They are simply killers.

As Christians we should be resolute about right and wrong. That is why ethics in the field is such a responsibility for us all. It has been said that character is what you are when no one is looking. When God gave mankind the Ten Commandments, they were to guide us in our decision making. Life is much easier when we don't have to reach a moral dilemma stage with every temptation we face. Our children learn their values from their parents. When they see a consistent model, they will begin to act out those values as their own. That's why taking children to explore the great outdoors is a first step in building a generation of hunters who will know the difference between right and wrong and will always act accordingly.

I have great respect for the law and for those who attempt to preserve it. However, if each of us lived by a code of doing what is right whatever the cost, we would have little need for law enforcement. People of character police themselves. I marvel when I look at all the fish and game laws in each state. However, those laws are necessary because of the swelling number of people who, left on their own, will not do the right thing. It makes life easier when those decisions are out of the way. Ethics are just as much a part of the outdoors as wearing hunter's orange and carrying a weapon.

The words "moral absolutes" are hated by this politically correct culture. It proudly announces to the world that right and wrong are not up for vote.

The time to make a decision is before you have to.

19

There are moral absolutes instituted by God for our own good. Our country is headed for a moral free fall because of our desire to have the final say about whether anything is right or wrong.

The time to make a decision is before you have to. Decide right now that you are going to live by an ethic that honors the Lord and elevates the preservation of our precious resources.

CHAPTER 7

Mysteries Afield

(Leave Room for Him to Work)

*For your thoughts are not my thoughts, neither
are your ways My ways, saith the Lord.*
—Isaiah 55:8

It is our nature to have a reason or explanation for everything that happens. Somehow that makes us feel as though we are in control. As people of faith, we know quite well that we must leave room for God to work on our behalf. Romans 8 says, "And we know that all things work together for good to them that love God, to them who are called according to His purpose."

> *As people of faith we know quite well that we must leave room for God to work on our behalf.*

Many years ago, I was preparing to hunt on some private acreage that had access to national forest land near Clarksville, Arkansas. There were few trees on this property. There was, however, a large hayfield. So I bought eight bales of hay and made a blind right in the middle of the field. The wait for bow season was over, and I carried my Browning Wasp recurve bow to my hay blind. When I arrived, it was obvious that someone had used my blind. This happened over and over. I would hike to the stand and see the bent-over grass and the wallowed-out area inside the blind.

Late one afternoon, I was headed to my spot, wondering who in the world was sneaking into my hidden fortress on private property. I eased up closer and saw some movement inside the bales of hay. I had him. Caught in the very act. As he stood up and stretched, I hid in the grass. This intruder had four legs and a huge set of antlers. The wily old buck loved my private suite. He enjoyed many afternoon naps concealed from the cares of life. I notched an arrow just as he winded me. The buck jumped the hay bales and the arrow that headed toward his vitals.

There are many mysteries in life. There are situations that are beyond our ability to figure out. From time to time we all ask, "Why?" "Why did this happen? Why now?" Perhaps the right question to ask during such times is "What now?" We must leave room for God to work. When bad things happen to good people, it unsteadies us all. It has been my duty hundreds of times to attempt to explain death or destruction to others. While working at the Joplin, Missouri, tornado site, my first task was to explain to a four-year-old girl and her grandmother that her daddy was lost in the rubble of the F-5 wreckage. I hate to be near people who are about to ask, "Why?" I seldom have the answer they need or want to hear. We must, however, always leave room for God to work.

I think I love the woods because they are full of things I cannot understand. I accept them by faith and just enjoy the fact that our great Creator has ways that I don't get. His thoughts are not my thoughts. I do know that, regardless of what we are going through in life, He is working all circumstances together that will be good for us in the end. Learning to wait on Him is our most difficult task. I will never be the hunter you read about in the record books. My picture will not be on the cover of hunting magazines. I seem to be more intrigued by what someone else is doing on my behalf than what I may do myself.

Hunting is a reflection of life. There are always questions, and eventually there will be answers. That has to be good enough for now. Our lives are to be lived out in the present. We cannot see into tomorrow, nor can we recreate yesterday. Jesus said, "Take therefore no thought for the morrow." Matthew 6:34 (KJV) When we worry about tomorrow, we make today even more difficult. I do not recommend that you carry your worry into the field. This is just not the place to bring anxiety. Too many things can go wrong. Focus is required when hunting.

Family vacations can sometimes end in disaster. The purpose of a getaway should be to find a new pace and to enjoy different things together. If we pack up all of our unresolved problems and unload them in vacationland, there is going to be trouble. Vacations should provide a communication level between family members that promote healing of our emotions. Even on vacation, leave room for God to work. Begin to make life changes that move toward resolution. Then peace may be found from your tree stand or the fishing hole. Always leave room for the Lord to work in every life situation.

After periods of stress or working through conflicts, a time-out in the woods is a great idea. Refocus is possible, and attention to the details of forest life returns. The mysteries of life are many, and sometimes the answers are few. Keep moving forward while you wait on the Lord. You will find that peace and harmony are closer than you imagined.

CHAPTER 8

Gadgets

(The Art of Instinct)

A young man was breaking into the world of hunting. He would go with me for short afternoon hunts or an occasional morning jaunt into the national forest. One morning we picked him up for a hunt. As he jumped in, an odor instantly drove us out of my pickup. I said, "What in the world is that smell?" He said, "I bought some Tinks 57. The man at the outdoor store said it would work great." That was a rough truck ride to the woods that day. My young friend didn't realize just where to apply Tinks 57.

I seldom watch hunting shows anymore, as they have turned into gadget getters. These pros hunt on land mostly inaccessible to regular folks. Their tips are always about buying more gadgets. While in a sporting goods store recently, I began counting all the products to spray on, drip from a tree, or throw on the ground. I finally quit counting, as there is just too much stuff to buy.

Anyone who will pay attention to the small details of life can hone their instincts

You cannot sell instinct. You cannot purchase common sense. I love to get tips that don't make me put one more thing in my pack. Dale Morrell, the archery target maker, taught me to shoot a compound bow. He gave me a great tip early one morning. He picked up a pocket full of acorns. Once in his tree, he would drop one, wait a little while, and drop another. A buck looking for breakfast would hear dropping acorns and come for a look. That's a great early season tip. Savvy hunters have instinct and common sense. They learn to be successful, whether they are on national forest land or an elite hunting club property, and they don't always use expensive gadgets.

Jesus said, "Behold, I send you forth as sheep in the midst of wolves, be ye therefore wise as serpents, and harmless as doves." Matthew 10:16 (KJV) The world has never been the believer's friend. The Lord gave us a great tip for dealing with the world. Be smart. That is instinct. Anyone who will pay attention to the small details of life can hone their instincts. When I was an associate pastor of a church, I would watch my senior pastor. If he was standing, I was standing. If he was visiting, I was visiting. If he was pulling weeds ... Well, you get it. I paid attention to the small details of ministry. Jesus told us, "He that is faithful in that which is least, is faithful also in much." Instinct is acquired by paying attention. A hunter who pays close attention to every sound and movement is a hunter who will create a good instinct for knowing when and where deer will move. Gadgets have little to do with success in anything. I would rather have an ounce of good instinct than a pack filled with gadgets.

Spiritual instinct is the ability to see through life situations and apply wisdom for the answer. Buy every translation of the Bible that you want, but only application of the Scriptures will bring solution.

As a sportsman, learn to rely upon your instincts. The gadget industry loves anything new, but your instincts will always reveal what is needed. Learn from those who have demonstrated great instinct. Watch closely those who have served the Lord a long time. They will reveal their secrets if you look closely.

A wise man once said that it takes 10,000 hours of training to be great at anything. If that is accurate, it amounts to over sixty weeks, which is about fourteen months of doing nothing but preparing for perfection. Since that is not a practical solution, I recommend spending your time by sharpening your skills and being faithful in the small things; it can bring great rewards.

Learn to find value in the small things in life. The tune of the songbirds from your stand or the antics of the squirrels sharing your tree may just be what you need to sharpen your instincts today.

CHAPTER 9

Stealth

(Oatmeal Pies Are Loud)

The person without the Spirit does not accept the
things that come from the Spirit of God but considers
them foolishness, and cannot understand them
because they are discerned only through the Spirit.
—1 Corinthians 2:14 (NIV)

We are all guilty. We have all done it. When attempting to have a Little Debbie Oatmeal Creme Pie while on the deer stand, we realized it is impossible to open one without alerting the entire woods that it's snack time. No matter how hard you try, you simply cannot be quiet while opening snacks that are factory packed.

As hunters, we worry about sound. Some sounds are natural. Limbs breaking off trees, acorns hitting the water, or ducks landing on a nearby lake—all are sounds that deer hear every day. They seldom give it a second look. But try to open a Little Debbie Oatmeal Cream Pie—my favorite, by the way—and you have concern. Plastic does not sound natural to the deer, nor does metal clanking of tree stands. Have you ever tried to prevent a sneeze while hunting? You can blow the top of your head off attempting that. The hunter brings to the woods sounds that are foreign to the natives.

Since it is our goal to enter the woods quietly and become stealth-like as we prepare for the hunt, it would be wise to organize your gear for that outcome. Opening a can of Vienna sausages or dropping your limb saw down the ladder is not a good stealth move.

We are right to be concerned about all the unnatural sounds that we bring into the woods. Smells are even worse. Cover scents are good, but stepping in a cow patty is even better, as it is natural to the deer. Natural sounds and smells do not alarm the forest critters that mankind has invaded their domain. It's the unnatural that usually brings the white flags out. Learning to walk quietly through the woods is an art. Practice walking in stealth mode. Put an old pair of socks over your boots if you are the stomping kind of traveler.

In 1 Corinthians 16:13 (KJV) The apostle Paul said, "Watch ye, stand fast in the faith, quit you like men, be strong." That is the Christian stealth mode. We are to operate in the world without calling attention to ourselves. Our job is to elevate Christ in every portion of our lives. That is natural. The unnatural for the believer is to make noise about their rights. The unnatural is to be a whiner about your life. We are to praise the Lord with every breath. That is natural. We alert the world when we gossip and whine about life or cut other believers down. We seem fake or phony to the world when we act and sound just like them.

We can eliminate our noisy tree stand behavior by placing our snacks in ziplock bags. We can organize our backpack to be quieter. We can learn to walk in stealth mode. We can mask our scent. We can learn to use the wind to our advantage. All of these actions will allow us to produce more natural sounds. That will get you to stealth mode. If only we worked that hard in our Christian lives, but that seems to be more difficult. Salvation brings transformation, and that is

> *While it only takes a moment to become a Christian, it takes a lifetime to become like Christ.*

instant. The behavioral changes come slower. We have to work on that all of our life. That is called sanctification. While it only takes a moment to become a Christian, it takes a lifetime to become like Christ. As believers we are to be dead to ourselves and to our old lives. That means we are not offended every day by criticism. That also means our personal rights are not worn on our sleeves.

One of the challenges of hunting is learning what is natural in the woods. Often we lament the fact that we must wear the hunter's orange vest and cap during gun hunting season. It does not look natural to us. But recently I had an eight-point buck walk up to within twenty yards of me. I was sitting on a log while complete in my orange outfit. Since I could not shoot, I remained in stealth mode. He grew tired of looking at me and changed direction. He never spooked or even blew at me. It all seemed natural to him. It is natural to be alert to spiritual danger. It is natural to be kind to others. It is natural to practice humility.

Live in the stealth mode, but enjoy your Little Debbie Oatmeal Creme Pies.

CHAPTER 10

Patience

(Passing Up Good for Best)

Whoever is patient has great understanding, but
one who is quick-tempered displays folly.
—Proverbs 14:29 (NIV)

Patience: the gift nobody ever asks for. We usually think of patience as an evil monster that is holding us against our will. However, if you desire to be known as a good hunter, you might as well sign up for patience 101 now. Sitting in the cold, blowing rain for hours in late November requires that you play the patience card. To get better at being a patient hunter, you must get better at being a patient person. James said, "Let patience have her perfect work, that ye may be perfect and entire wanting nothing." James 1:4 (KJV) This is an admonishment for us to allow patience to complete its mission. For that to happen, we must keep our emotions in check during the process. Our response to the bad things that happen to us determines how long the patience course may need to last. A hunter that can endure difficulties will often be rewarded for their patience.

Patience is not just about enduring the bad times. It is also about passing up a good opportunity for a better one. If you always shoot the first legal buck that shows up, you will never get a chance to harvest a better one.

This is a lesson in not being a prisoner of patience but rather its partner. The first time I decided to pass on shooting a buck was a lesson on partnering with myself to wait for something better. When patience completes its work in us, we have a better perspective about life. If we can wait on the good while expecting the better, we might even get to see the best.

To achieve a God-centered life requires deep patience. Life can throw some pretty hard fastballs. Our response to bad things happening can prepare us for greater endurance. Patience is designed by God for our good. If we cannot handle the normal pressures of life, then navigating the extreme pain and pressure that comes our way will be impossible. Patience is God's final filter for endurance.

A patient hunter is usually a skilled hunter. Remaining focused when weather conditions are impossible takes patience. Remaining focused when your family is in crisis takes patience. When you lose all that you hold dear, as Job did, only patience can bring you back from the edge. Job attended ten funerals in one day. All of his children died in a terrible terrorist raid. "Yet in all this Job sinned not." Job 1:22 (KJV) It is hard to be patient when life seems to have conspired against you. Job learned that patience does not change your circumstances; it only makes them palatable. When dark days like Job endured come our way, patience should be the first weapon of choice.

Patience is a virtue. It causes us to grow up. It reframes our thinking. It allows us to go beyond our normal comfort zones. If patience could be achieved by a textbook or classes, then it would not have the impact that it has upon our lives. We learn patience largely through problems. We can also learn patience by passing on things that are good in order to have opportunity for things that are best. We live in an instant-gratification culture. Waiting is simply not an option. Saving for a purchase takes too long, so just charge it. Making payments is more satisfying than saving because it requires patience to save for anything. A young store clerk asked me recently if I wanted to apply for their company credit card. When I declined, he asked why I didn't want more credit. I replied, "Credit doesn't make us wealthy. Money does. Saving money—not applying for credit cards—creates wealth." It requires a lot of patience to build wealth in a culture that places no value on it.

> *This is not just about being a more successful hunter. It is about being a more successful human.*

This is not just about being a more successful hunter. It is about being a more successful human. Hunting is merely a reflection of life. If you can learn to be patient with those who are not patient with you, then you can learn to endure some uncomfortable circumstances when you are on an outdoor adventure. Your greatest weapon is not a bow or gun. It is the ability to show patience when everyone else has lost theirs.

I would like to say that I am a naturally patient person; however, that is just not the case. Patience is a learned process. Many good people are pushed to the limit in life and stay on their feet. They have learned that this process can be brutal, but necessary. Patience and hard times carpool together. When couples endure a hardship and work through it, they have a more stable relationship. They are always close by each other. As you learn God's purpose, remember that patience is your gift to navigate life. That is only possible when you partner with patience.

Hunting and fishing are not always about a 150-class buck or an eight-pound bass. They form a postgraduate course in patience and perseverance. It is learning that the process of life has greater value to us when we wait on the Lord.

CHAPTER 11

Anticipation

(Road Trips and Dip Cones)

Then Joshua said to the people, "Consecrate yourselves,
for tomorrow the Lord will do wonders among you."
—Joshua 3:5

Our family began planning a trip to Disney World more than a year in advance of the departure time. The grandchildren peaked a little too soon with their anticipation—about six months too soon. Sometimes, the anticipation of an event can be better than the event itself. In many instances, the event becomes a letdown because of the high expectations placed in our mind by anticipation.

The reality is that life seldom ever lives up to the anticipation that precedes it.

If you have ever booked a hunt with a guide, you had expectations. The moment that money changed hands, you began to expect that you would have a good chance to harvest a nice trophy. In essence, the money that you gave to the outfitter was to purchase a fair chase opportunity. While we know that is true, anticipation does not operate within boundaries. Our mind will use imagination to move past the confines of reality. That's why children are prone to high levels of anticipation.

The reality is that life seldom ever lives up to the anticipation that precedes it. Marriages end in divorce because of disappointment. It is said that the number one emotion felt by Americans is disillusionment. Proverbs 15:22 says, "Without counsel, purposes are disappointed, but in the multitude of counselors there is safety." The counselors in our lives are there to remind us that there can be a gap between reality and anticipation.

Hunting has a huge anticipation factor. Will there be a good restaurant while we travel? Will the lodging be comfortable? Will I have the opportunity of a lifetime to get my scope on a monster buck? That is just the beginning. It is human nature to desire things to go well. That is true in every area of our lives. Anticipation has to be tempered with reality. When you let anticipation run wild, you will usually be disappointed with the outcome of any life event.

Many years ago, my son Shawn, along with fellow church member and hunting friend Tim Wise, booked a two-day hunt down in the black belt country of Alabama. The long drive led us into the huge dark woods of the black belt. When we finally arrived at the small lodge, three men were walking out with their gear. The young outfitter stuck out his hand and gave a farewell to the three slump-shouldered hunters. His final sentence to them was "I wish you guys would have been here last week. The deer were really moving." With that, the three loaded up their truck and headed for home. Anticipation level for us fell to the floor with that outfitter's parting words to the other hunters.

Two days later, we were walking out to load our gear and head toward Arkansas. As we were loading, a pickup pulled into the drive. Four men jumped from their truck and asked, "Did you guys kill any nice ones?" Our sad reply deflated their anticipation. I knew their feeling. The outfitter came through the door, and here were his parting words for us: "I wish you guys could be here next week. I think the deer are gonna really start moving."

Anticipation can be a friend or foe. In life there are things beyond our control. We can remain positive about the bad things that happen to us. We can also develop a bad attitude and become resentful or bitter when things don't work out the way we wanted them to. The only way that you can be promised a trophy buck is to hunt in a fenced area where your money will always meet your anticipation. It is guaranteed. Fair chase in hunting means that you only have opportunity. Fair chase in life means the same thing. You will be given opportunity. I have learned how to keep anticipation in check through many disappointments. It's just best not to believe all the hype that comes with every opportunity.

Life is life. It brings joy and sadness. It brings success as well as failure. If we can learn to enjoy the road trips of life, we will have fewer conflicts with disappointment. When I see a Dairy Queen while on a road trip, I am thinking, *Large dip cone!* Soft ice cream dipped into hot chocolate on a cone starts my anticipation levels moving. The simple things in life seldom disappoint. They are not designed to change your life or sweep you off your feet. They just offer a small distraction from normal.

A walk in the woods with your spouse on a beautiful fall morning can change the dynamic of an entire day. The more money you spend on enjoying anything, the more expectation you will have. The more expectation you have, the more likely you are to be let down. I love road trips and dip cones, but I have learned that flat tires happen on road trips and dip cones cannot always be found.

> Disappointment to a noble soul is what cold
> water is to burning metal; it strengthens,
> tempers, intensifies, but never destroys it
> —Eliza Tabor

CHAPTER 12

Trust

(The Building Block of Community)

But I trust in your unfailing love; my
heart rejoices in your salvation.
—Psalm 13:5

A few years ago while elk hunting in Colorado, an unusual thing happened to me. I parked my four-wheeler at the edge of a dark woods area. These areas are difficult to navigate on foot because of all the dead fall. I spent several hours working my way through the area. When I came out on the other side of the dark woods, I was met by a natural draw that elk were using. I positioned myself about fifty yards up on the side of the draw.

> *Trust is the big issue in life. Every relationship is either strengthened by trust or destroyed by the lack of it.*

It was well past lunch, so I got my sandwich, chips, and Little Debbie Oatmeal Creme Pie out to enjoy a little rest and wait for a bull to come through the draw. I was nestled against a fir tree among the low-hanging boughs. That's when I first saw him. He was sitting on a branch in another fir tree about fifteen feet away from me. This strange little bird was staring me down.

He was gray with a little black line along his side. He had the most curious look in his black eyes.

The little bird had my full attention. He watched me with great interest as I ate my sandwich. I took a pinch of bread crust and sat it on the tree limb beside me. It took him about thirty seconds to make up his mind. He flew down right beside the crust, picked it up in his beak, and returned to his branch. We repeated that process three times. Then, in a flash, he was gone. I thought how amazing that exchange had been. I finished my sandwich and was about to enjoy my oatmeal creme pie when he returned to his tree branch. However, he was not alone. He brought two of his pals with him. I am a student of animal behavior. Their ability to communicate can be uncanny. How was that little bird now named Moe able to communicate to Larry and Curly that he had found a vending machine for birds? They had to trust him to follow blindly. Trust is the big issue in life. Every relationship is either strengthened by trust or destroyed by the lack of it.

I have trusted Christ for my salvation, but I also trust Him with my life. I am in His hands. He is the potter; I am the clay. I trust Him through every trial and conflict. "Those who know your name will trust in you, for you Lord, has never forsaken those who seek you." Trust is a character trait that is often lost on this culture. It is our responsibility to act accordingly when people trust us. My wife trusts me to be faithful to her. My children trust me to always guide them with truth. When we run from those duties, trust is lost. When trust is lost, so is the relationship. It can take years to rebuild trust.

Back to Moe, Larry, and Curly. I pinched off a bite of my Little Debbie and placed it on the limb. Moe came right over and took the bite to Larry and Curly. Well, my nature is to go with the flow, so I placed three bites of my ever-shrinking snack on the limb. Moe was back in a flash, but Larry and Curly just sat frozen on the limb. They were having none of it. Moe had led them to the buffet but he could not instill trust in them. Trust can take time to build, but only an instant to destroy. God is faithful, even in our disobedience. His love for us is unconditional. To trust the Lord is to leave your future with Him.

My story of trust comes to a close with a final observation about my friend Moe. I was losing light and had a long trek back through the dark woods, so I got my GPS bearings and started through the timber. When I finally got to the four-wheeler, I sat down for a drink of water and to prepare for a long four-wheeler ride back to the cabin. Just as I was about to leave, three birds landed in a tall pine beside the ATV. I could not believe my eyes. Moe, Larry, and Curly had followed me all the way back. I told Moe that I had nothing else to give him. I think Moe trusted me for what he could get from me.

That can be said of many Christians also. To follow Christ for what we can gain is a selfish motive. Trust must be from the heart. Jesus did not die on the cross to ensure you a prosperous and successful life. His death was to pay the debt of sin that every human being carries. His death transforms us from sinners without hope into saints who are powered by His Holy Spirit. I trust Christ. I guess the larger question is "Does He trust me?"

Sometimes when I reflect back on that day, I am convinced that God used Moe as a teaching point in my life. He reminded me through that eye-opening experience that I can trust the Lord, not just for salvation but also for the next breath. Tomorrow's sunrise is way over my pay grade to understand, so I guess I'd better trust that to Him as well.

CHAPTER 13

Legacy

(Leaving Life Better than We Found It)

"The legacy you leave is the life you lead." When I read that statement, it always has impact. The idea of leaving something behind for others begins to take hold as we age and we recognize our own vulnerability. Every lover of the great outdoors owes a debt to those who came before us. They created national parks to protect our treasures for posterity. They developed hunting areas in every state that would allow the wild game to prosper. With the purchase of every hunting license, we are leaving legacy for the next generation to enjoy.

I have three grown children and eight grandchildren. I am not a wealthy person, so legacy has to come in the form of teaching my family that the rich traditions like hunting and fishing have to be carefully protected. When a family holds a value of loving and caring for our woods and waterways, they also by nature will care for one another. It cannot always be about harvesting a trophy. Legacy needs workdays. Days that you invest into the land to help preserve its natural state. When I see aluminum cans and Doritos bags along trails, it is upsetting. How can people just drop trash in a pristine area and walk away? Our beautiful lakes and rivers need policing as more and more people use them without caring for them. Legacy can be taking a day to clean up a state park. Our park systems work hard to keep these treasures clean, but it's just too massive of a job.

While teaching a kayak course on the Buffalo National River near Ponca, Arkansas, I realized that if I don't take an active role in picking up the cans and the paper, we won't have these treasures in the future. Teaching my grandchildren that it's their responsibility to keep it clean is my duty. America is unique. We still have a wonderful system in place of hunting, fishing, and exploring that is unmatched in the world. Even with all the current negative rhetoric about guns, our future is bright. Responsible citizens all over this country protect and defend the rights of all of us to enjoy the natural resources that God has given us.

Our great need is to love these areas by our actions. Another legacy we can leave is to introduce children to the world of hunting and fishing. So many children grow up without a father in their home. They are not privileged to hike a mountain trail or sit in a boat and catch a fish. You can make a difference in a child's life by investing your time and dollars into teaching them these skills. There are many clubs and organizations that offer these services. When we give our time to a boy or girl by introducing them to the great outdoors, we open a door of opportunity for them that will never close. They will have a new perspective about their anger. They will see that the world is so much larger than they realized. Troubles have a way of vanishing when we breathe in the freshness of a mountain stream or sit under the stars on a crisp autumn evening. Children can learn self-control and independence when they embrace the outdoor lifestyle. I love to sit around an evening campfire and let kids talk. They will ask questions about life when they allow their emotional walls to fall around them.

If we can teach children to take responsibility for their actions, we can build a future generation that will become leaders in outdoor conservation. When boys and girls are taught ethical behavior in the field, they will live by it in their lives. Teens are starving for a hero today. The PlayStation generation finds it difficult to sort reality from fantasy. Harvesting an animal is real. A life is taken. There is reality in this process. Butchering the meat so that none is wasted is also part of the growing-up process for young hunters.

Legacy is more than leaving money for others to remember your name. It is leaving your life behind in the lives of those coming after you. We will all leave something behind. In fact, we will leave it all behind. You must be intentional in your efforts of changing a culture by changing one life at a time. Today I asked three boys if they had been able to go hunting at all this season. All three said, "No, but we would love too. Would you take us?"

> *You must be intentional in your efforts of changing a culture by changing one life at a time.*

Kids are so willing to explore the unknown. It is part of the imagination God gives to them. Our mission as adults should include giving boys and girls an opportunity to sit around a campfire after a hunt or fishing trip and retell their story by the firelight.

A couple of years ago, my wife, Jan, and I were trout fishing on the Norfork River in northern Arkansas with our oldest grandson, Dakota. I was fortunate to catch a six-pound German brown trout. It was a memorable battle. After I released the brown back into the cold water, Dakota said, "Papaw, we will never forget this day as long as we live." I pray he is right. "A good man leaves an inheritance to his children's children."

CHAPTER 14

Bull's-eye

(The Skill of Not Missing)

Hitting the bull's-eye is the perfection of the shot. Whether gun, bow, or rod, the knack of hitting what you are aiming at is crucial. Competitive shooters will fire thirty to fifty thousand rounds each year to keep their edge. They hit the bull's-eye because they are relentless in their quest to be perfect. They judge themselves harshly in their failure because so much rides on every shot. For the rest of us, we just try to get close.

Jan and I were fishing on the Yellowstone River with the Montana Trout Scout, Craig Beam. Using nine-foot fly rods, we were casting hoppers to the outer edge of the bank and having them fall right at the water's edge. Hitting the mark while moving swiftly downstream in a drift boat was challenging. Hitting the mark is always difficult. The goal was not just getting the fly there; it was to hook a big rainbow or German brown. Learning the skill of presentation made those opportunities possible.

> *No amount of practice or work can change the fact that apart from the love of God there is no answer for our sin.*

Real-life situations make perfection a stranger. I can stand thirty yards from a Morrell bag target in my yard and place arrows in a tight group all day long. Climb twenty feet up and tie yourself to an oak tree with the wind blowing at twenty miles an hour, however, and it's a whole new game. Practicing your shots in harsh weather conditions gives your aim an advantage. I learned to fire the M-16A1 rifle in the army. I fired that weapon so many times that I had a fixed sense of where every shot was going to go. That weapon could shoot a twenty-round clip faster than an automatic shotgun could pump out three shots. So our motto was "Just get close." No hunter should ever take a weapon to the field without having great confidence in placing rounds exactly where they are looking.

The time came to see how proficient I was with my M-16. Our graduation from boot camp was now down to hitting the bull's-eye. I made it through every section of the shooting test with a quiet resolve. The final portion had the long-distance pop-up targets that were four feet tall. Looking over three hundred yards down range, the four-foot targets looked like they were twelve inches tall. The instructor whispered to me that I only had to hit three of these targets to qualify for the expert ribbon. My confidence level was off the chart. The targets fell and I was awarded the expert medal upon graduation. Confidence is vital when you fire, and confidence is built through practice.

There is a spiritual truth to this subject. To miss the mark is called sin. "For all have sinned and come short of the glory of God." Romans 3:23(KJV) This malady is universal. We are all sinners. "For there is none righteous, no not one." There is a remedy for our sin. An atonement was made by Jesus Christ. His blood was shed so that we could have peace with God. No amount of practice or work can change the fact that apart from the love of God, there is no answer for our sin. John 3:16 (KJV) says "For God so loved the world that He gave His only begotten son that whosoever believes in Him shall not perish, but have everlasting life."

God's grace is greater than all our sin. You will never be beyond the need of grace. "For by grace are you saved, and that not of yourselves, it is the gift of God and not of works lest any man should boast." Ephesians 2:8 (KJV)

Forgiveness is the result of confessing our sins to God. Our confession to God about our sin is the foundation of our testimony. Our lives are reframed by this fact. We can forgive others because we have been forgiven.

We have all made bad shots before. It happens. Usually when we miss a shot, we look at our weapon as though to say, "What happened? I had perfect aim." It is almost always true that when we miss, it is operator failure. In life, the miss is in our nature. We are sinners by a nature that must be redeemed, and Jesus conquered our sin and death when He rose from the dead, providing our redemption.

Strive to become a good shot. Practice with diligence to land your lure where it needs to go. Build your confidence with every shot. Hitting the bull's-eye never comes easy. There must be sweat equity involved if you want to possess the skill to hit the mark.

CHAPTER 15

Memories

(Flashbacks of Life)

By the rivers of Babylon, there we sat down
and wept, when we remembered Zion.
—Psalm 137:1

M y childhood was a combination of boyhood adventures and deep family heartache. Over time our mind has a way to soften the memories of things that almost crushed us, while highlighting the exhilarating memories. God has reserved a portion of our brain for recalling memories. Without this function, the human soul loses its moorings. Children who lose the anchor of family traditions also lose the value systems that keep a family strong during difficult times. As we replay events from our past mentally, we are reminded of mistakes that we do not want to repeat. At will, you can recall your favorite

> *Over time our mind has a way to soften the memories of things that almost crushed us, while highlighting the exhilarating memories.*

childhood Christmas or relive a past hunt or the release of a trophy fish. No computer ever created can surpass our God-given ability to store and recall life.

Our country is in great peril. There are terrorists who want to create an environment of fear. There are socialists who want to remove our Second Amendment rights. There are politically correct activists who are rewriting the future by destroying our past. All of these groups pose a threat to freedom. However, our greatest foe is the breakdown of the family. Family used to extend itself outward. We talked at the kitchen table. We laughed and cried together. Our homes were small, and the kids shared rooms. We had one family car. We went to town together. An entire afternoon was spent cutting down a cedar tree and dragging it home to decorate for Christmas. We went to church. There was no children's department, and there were no student pastors. There were no family life centers. The whole family went to church together and came home. Sunday dinner was a favorite memory for me. Smelling pan-fried chicken cooking while anticipating my grandma's apple pie still makes my mouth water.

While yesterday's family extended outward, today's family retreats inward. Children separate themselves from family with their video games. Every child has his or her own room. Many families drive two different cars to church. Even at church we break the family apart. We seldom do anything as family. This inward pull lessens the influence of family. I do not think we will reverse this trend in family until we intentionally think and act outwardly again. Today, the theme for the American family seems to be escape. Our past families had nothing to escape from, nor a place to escape to.

I was born at Paris, Arkansas, in 1952. My parents then moved us to California. My father had survived World War II and Korea as a soldier in the army. He suffered greatly from PTSD. No one talked about that in those days, and there was no help for returning soldiers. Dad became an alcoholic. Our family suffered together. One morning my mother loaded my sister, Jackie, and me, along with our unborn brother, Steve, into our uncle's huge Buick and headed us toward Arkansas. That road trip was filled with exciting things to see. We followed Route 66 across America. We were never to see our dad again. That long journey was followed by meeting my grandparents. My sister and I stood at the front door of their little house in Arkansas and knocked. A large-framed man of over six feet answered the knock. His stature was overwhelming. I asked him, "Are you my grandfather?" That began a six-year period in our lives that was secure and adventure-filled for me.

When I was almost eleven years old, my grandfather suffered a heart attack and died. There were no good-byes or parting words of love. He was just gone. Our family came unraveled. He was eighty-six when he died. He and my little brother, Steve, were inseparable. Since my brother had never seen our dad, Granddad was both dad and grandfather rolled into one. We milked the cows together. Gathering the eggs and slopping the hogs were daily chores with Granddad.

I never went deer hunting in my life until I was grown. There were no memories of anticipating the next morning hunt. But my granddad instilled many traditions that are still a part of family for us today. When I see Christmas hams in the store, I instantly go back in my mind to our smokehouse and hear granddad say, "Okay, Bobby, you pick the ham we are gonna eat for Christmas dinner." When I see the baking hens in the meat market, I can remember Granddad killing ten chickens on the chopping block in one morning. That one still haunts me a little, seeing ten headless bodies flopping all over the ground.

This chapter is not about hunting or fishing. It's about what makes them both great: the power of memory. This culture is consumer based. What I mean by that is that we are a generation of takers. We take what we want without giving thought to giving. Everything, even church, is a consumer-based lifestyle. Memories take time. None of us seem to have any of that. We are successful. We have more cars in our driveway than we have licensed drivers. Our love for things has overshadowed our desire to slow down and make memories.

In Philippians 1:3(KJV) Paul said, "I thank my God upon every remembrance of you." He wrote this from his prison cell. In his difficult situation, he used the memories of his past to keep himself encouraged. You are blessed with the treasure of memory. Invest your time in the next generation to ensure that with all their getting, they get some great memories of family.

I recall an elk-hunting trip to the Flattop Wilderness Area of Colorado. Steve and his son, Stevie, along with my son, Shawn, found a little roadside cafe that was open at 3 a.m. We were exhausted and had several more hours to drive. My brother went to the restroom, and while he was gone, I told the young man who was both cook and waiter that my brother was very hard of hearing. I asked him if he could please speak very loudly when talking to him. I also told him that he needed to be very close to his face while talking to him. The young man said that he understood. When my brother returned to the stool at the counter, the young man leaned over the bar right in Steve's face and almost screamed, *"What can I get you to eat?"* They sat there screaming at each other while the rest of us were exploding with laughter. Every time I recall that memory, I think of my brother and smile.

Look at every hunting and fishing trip as an opportunity to place a new memory on the hard drive of your mind. Memories, whether good or bad, are vitally important to remember why life is so precious.

CHAPTER 16

Weather

(Baby, It's Cold Outside)

In journeyings often, in perils of waters, in perils
of robbers, in perils of my own countrymen...
2 Corinthians 11:26 (KJV)

My first elk hunt found Shawn and me in Craig, Colorado, during the final gun season. Our reason for choosing that season was the advice of a hunter from Minnesota who had experienced success there the year before. We packed and planned for days. This area allowed four-wheelers so they were loaded on our trailer along with our tent and all the gear. Finally, we were ready for the road trip.

Craig is a small town in northern Colorado, about a thirty-minute drive to the Wyoming border. The final gun season is right before Thanksgiving, so that meant it would be bitterly cold. This particular season can be successful if there is enough snow to drive the elk herds off the mountain and into their wintering grounds. Now cold in Colorado is not the same as cold in Arkansas. We arrived in Craig three days before the season began in order to do some scouting. We purchased a few last-minute items, grabbed a bite of lunch, and studied the topo maps. With great anticipation, we left the quaint little town and headed to the Bureau of Land of Management area to set up our camp. Snow and sleet fell on us the entire day. The weather report predicted that the snow was going to be heavy in the area.

By the time we made camp, the temperature had plummeted and we were in a whiteout condition. Bone-chilling winds were wreaking havoc with our tent. All of our food and water was frozen. The only thing not frozen is what we had in our ice chest! The November storm was welcoming us to Colorado. The first night of our Elk Hunt was miserable. I have never known cold like this before. Conditions continued to deteriorate. The blizzard finally won. We deserted our camp and drove to Baggs, Wyoming. The little town of four hundred people offered a truck stop, gas station, motel, and cafe. Baggs is located in the infamous Carbon County, where Butch Cassidy and his Wild Bunch gang had a hideout cabin in the 1890s. We headquartered there with a few stranded truckers.

When the storm finally broke, we returned to our camp and had one day to scout before the season began. While the blizzard had moved out of the area, the high winds and low temps remained. Shawn got on the trail of a migrating herd of elk and followed them until he was exhausted. Up to this point, the trip of a lifetime had been one challenge after another. That night we went to bed at five o'clock in the afternoon, because the only warm place we could find was in our mummy sleeping bags. I remember being zipped in that bag with nothing but my eyes and nose exposed. Our tent had transitioned into an igloo. The winds were so fierce that the flapping of our tent sounded like a helicopter trying to land on top of us. I turned to my son and said, "You know, I have never been depressed in my life, but I am getting awfully close now."

We survived the long night and drove back into Craig the next day. An old-time outdoor storeowner we had met earlier told us we should find Godiva Rim and hunt in that area. That was forty miles across the mountain. We deserted our camp for a second time and found a small motel. It was the last available room in the entire town. We got up opening morning and drove forty miles across the mountain to a place we had never seen before. The winds were quiet on that cold morning. Hiking through the snow, I found a small trail that circled some huge, ancient, volcanic boulders. The area was being used by elk so I set up in a thicket of cedars and sage bushes. As soon as I got comfortable, the snow began to fall. Not in a blizzard fashion this time, just a beautiful quiet snow. The world seemed at peace. I had poured a cup of coffee and was enjoying a little Debbie Oatmeal Creme Pie as I watched the snow gently drift over the sage.

The silence was broken when Shawn called and said, "I need help." It was only about nine o'clock in the morning. When I finally found him across the valley, he was sitting beside a beautiful six-by-six bull. We spent the next three hours skinning and quartering the elk. We were back to the motel that afternoon and crashed for the remainder of the day.

Early on the second day, we made the forty-mile trip back to the Godiva Rim. Our trek in the snow led us to a thick cover of cedars. The world seemed to be sound asleep. The wind was slight from the northwest. We set up on the outside edge of the cover, facing a clearing. Shawn spotted a bull running right at us. He sounded like a bulldozer crashing through the woods. Someone had spooked the bull higher up on the ridge. I took the shot as he ran past us. Again we began the grueling work of field dressing an elk in two feet of snow. By 10 a.m. on the second day of the season, we had both tagged out. We drove back across the mountain, loaded up our camp, and prepared for a long night drive to Alma, Arkansas. Another snowstorm moved in on us, and all the way to Denver, we traveled at twenty-five miles an hour.

Whenever I am cold I think, this is still not Colorado cold. There was a spiritual lesson gained from that trip. It really doesn't matter how a thing begins, but how it ends is vitally important. It was an awesome experience for us to drive eight hundred miles and hunt in an area we had never seen. It was even better that we both tagged an elk and headed home on the second night of the season. Those are memories that I replay often. The impact of that adventure, however, was the hardship of just hanging on when everything

> *It really doesn't matter how a thing begins, but how it ends is vitally important.*

is going wrong. The struggles of life can bend us until we almost break. The sun will shine again; we just have to hang on. The struggle becomes the journey, and the journey becomes the memory.

If we knew in advance of the conflicts we must face, we would never leave the security of our homes. Fear would paralyze us. The life lessons that come our way often come with a high price. The only thing worse than having to go through a difficult trial is to go through it and learn nothing from it.

God is not done with you yet. "Being confident of this very thing, that He which hath begun a good work in you will perform it until the day of Jesus Christ." Philippians 1:6 (KJV)

CHAPTER 17

The Magic Corn Tree

(The Gift of Provision)

> Look at the birds of the air, that they do not sow, nor
> reap nor gather into barns, and yet your Heavenly Father
> feeds them. Are you not worth much more than they?
> —Matthew 6:26

I was in a box blind in Kansas, deer hunting with Steve Malone, a deacon in our church. It was 6:44 a.m. on a cold December morning. A couple does moved into the clearing. They grazed a few minutes and moved closer to the magic corn tree. Right at 7 a.m., the corn feeder automatically discharged the corn. Within moments, five more doe eased into the area and began eating the corn. As the sun got higher, more animals moved into the clearing. A young buck came in and was feeding when another small group of does came back into the feeding area. The winds changed and the deer coming in were beginning to catch our scent. Around noon, a nice eleven-point buck and a couple of does moved into the feeding area. While we passed on the buck, it had been an amazing morning. Twenty-two deer had come by to graze on the corn by lunchtime.

I began to think, *Do these deer ever question the magic corn tree, or do they just accept the fact that two times every day corn will fall to the ground?* After the deer had moved on, blue jays and cardinals dined at the feeder. Red squirrels, raccoons, and opossums also benefitted from the corn tree. The animals didn't call a meeting questioning the provision. They just enjoyed it and moved on. It was interesting to watch the deer coming in before the feeder released the corn. They knew from experience that the yellow corn would be provided.

Some states outlaw the feeding of game animals. I am in favor of the practice because it provides better nutrition to the animals during harsh winter months. It also serves as a prenatal supplement to pregnant does. I struggle, however, with hunters who come into the sport thinking that deer hunting is simply setting up a feeder and a tree stand. There is so much more to learning the outdoor skills needed to be a good hunter. It is not a lazy-person sport. Scouting for deer movement requires miles of walking. Setting stands in a hunting area is hard work. A hunter's chance of harvesting an animal goes up in proportion to the amount of work that went into the process. Sometimes we may get lucky, but for the most part, our luck is the hard work that goes into preparing for the hunt.

A few states do not allow baiting or feeding of any kind due to the chronic wasting disease in animals that is now affecting herds in as many as seventeen states and two Canadian provinces. The disease is complicated and new research from the University of Texas indicates there are many reasons besides baiting for the existence of CWD.

The concept of provision is a spiritual one. "But my God shall supply all your need according to His riches in glory by Christ Jesus." Philippians 4:19 (KJV) As Christians we pray for the Lord to meet our needs. Jesus said in Matthew 6:9-13 (NIV), "This then is how you should pray, Our Father which art in heaven, hallowed by thy name. Thy kingdom come thy will be done on earth as it is in heaven. Give us this day our daily bread." To ask for God's help to meet our need is natural. It is the appropriate response for every believer. The more that we trust the Lord to meet today's need, the easier it is to trust Him for the unknown future.

I have always loved observing the behavior of animals. Each day brings to them a new set of circumstances. They learn to navigate the storms that quickly change their environment. Heat, cold, and wind are daily encounters for the animal kingdom. Animals are not made in the image of God, so there is no spirit of gratitude. They do not say, "Praise the Lord," when they find food. The ability to give thanks for provision separates us from the animals. American Indian hunters after harvesting an animal would thank the animal for its life. Their gratitude was demonstrated by using every part of the animal to sustain their way of life.

When someone says, "thank you," they are demonstrating the most Godly of acts...gratitude.

As believers, we should always have a spirit of gratitude for God's provision. It is the most natural thing we can do. "In everything give thanks for this is the will of God in Christ Jesus concerning you." 1 Thessalonians 5:18 (KJV) Each time I leave the woods or make my final cast, I thank the Lord for the experience. When someone says, "Thank you," they are demonstrating the most godly of acts: gratitude. Whether we harvest a buck or we come home empty-handed, our best response is always "Lord, I thank you." Children are conditioned to be thankful for what they get. When they become aware of God's provision, their response grows into a thanks for what He has given.

Wouldn't it be nice if we had a magic corn tree? In a way, we do: God's provision. While the Lord is faithful to us, it is not magic; it is grace. There is always a way to praise the Lord for His goodness to us.

CHAPTER 18

Sunrise

(The Genesis of Life)

The LORD is righteous in her midst,
He will do no unrighteousness.
Every morning He brings His justice to light;
He never fails,
But the unjust knows no shame.
—Zephaniah 3:5 NKJV

Everything is better at sunrise. When the final moments of darkness yield to the eastern sky, the day begins. The genesis of life happens when the sun takes its rightful place. It's as though the world begins each morning when daylight comes. The animals even seem to enjoy this special time of day. The hunter on the stand is warmed as the sun climbs on its western path. It's all part of God's gift to mankind. Even on nonhunting days, these are magical moments.

Growing up on my granddad's farm, starting to work before sunrise was a normal practice. Milking cows, feeding the hogs, and gathering eggs were often completed just about the time the sun would bring light to the world. My granddad loved to start the day with a can-do attitude. I understood that work was a natural thing, as natural as the sunrise itself. After the morning chores, granddad would take out his pocket watch and say, "Let's see if Granny has cooked us up some eggs." Breakfast was our first break of the day. There was a natural rhythm as work and rest exchanged places through the course of the day.

Sunrise for the outdoorsman is a magical time. Casting a line on the water at daylight is poetry in motion. Fish like the daily genesis as well. Rising from the depths to attack a top-water lure or fly brings the ultimate one-on-one battle. Releasing a beautiful rainbow back to its pristine waters at daylight is every fisherman's dream. There is no way to describe the captured moments of daylight. They come and go every twenty-four hours. They provide for us a new opportunity to begin life. Many people take a pass on watching the sun make its daily entrance, choosing rather to hit the snooze button. I do not really understand the science of it, but I somehow feel that I am getting a jumpstart on the world if I beat the sun to work. One fundamental principle of leadership is to start the day early. Good leaders recognize that in order to develop other people, they must first take time to develop themselves. To do that requires meeting the sunrise.

> *Good leaders recognize that in order to develop other people they must first take time to develop themselves.*

I have seen the sunrise over the Pacific, Atlantic, and Indian oceans. I have seen it make an entrance on the Himalayan Mountains. My family once sat on the rim of the Grand Canyon and watched the rising sun create a plethora of color in that vast gorge. It doesn't matter where I witness the sunrise; it always has the same effect on me. I think as I watch it, *Lord, you did it again.*

I was deer hunting in the national forest near Clarksville, Arkansas, with my brother Steve. It was a frosty morning, the winds were calm, but the air had a bite to it. It was one of those mornings when you think the sun is just never going to show itself. Almost on cue, the shining yellow ball rose to the sounds of dogs chasing a nice buck. Sunrise made this chase visible. Back and forth, the buck worked to escape the yelping hounds. The chase went on for minutes when finally I caught a glimpse of the buck. He was a wide-rack eight-point beauty. The woods were dense with many small bushes underneath the large pine trees. Getting a shot was going to be difficult and the hounds closing in continued to push the deer for thicker cover. I kept thinking that my brother may just get a shot off as the buck continued to move his way. We were both in tree stands about seventy yards apart. The cold predawn darkness had given way to the warmth of the sun. I put my field glasses up quickly to see the buck inching toward my brother's stand, and in the same picture was my brother sound asleep on the stand. The morning sun can make even the most hard-core hunter sleepy. I have enjoyed a few sunrise naps myself. We did not harvest a buck that day, but we sure made a sunrise memory.

King David's final words were "and He shall be as the light of the morning, when the sun riseth, even a morning without clouds; as the tender grass springing out of the earth by clear shining after rain." 2 Samuel 23:4 (KJV) These words are spoken by the king about God. The first light of the morning is symbolic to the presence of God in our lives. God is light. He has called us to be light as well. It's good practice for us to be up early enough each day to see how God does it. We cannot produce light, but we can reflect it. Our job is to reflect to others the light that is shining on us. I will always be a sunrise guy. And I guess I will always believe that if I get started on the day at sunrise, I just may be the first to having my rod bent double or a buck in my sights.

"From the rising of the sun unto the going down of the same, the Lord's name is to be praised." Psalm 113:3 (KJV)

CHAPTER 19

Small Things

(Savoring the Insignificant)

For who has despised the day of small things?
—Zechariah 4:10

On Christmas morning 1963, an eleven-year-old boy went through his gifts in a flash. The usual orange and apple along with candy canes in the stocking were laid aside. The one thing he was looking for was not there. The only present under the tree was a bill cap with earflaps. He tried to not show his disappointment and worked hard at holding back the tears. For more than a year, he had dreamed of owning his own rifle. He knew the chances were slim due to the difficult time the family was having after the loss of his grandfather. Dreaming, however, was never a struggle for him. After the presents were opened, his mom said she had left something in the backseat of the car. The disappointed young boy slowly walked to the car and looked in the back seat. He saw a blanket on the floor. Removing the blanket, he could not believe what he saw. There it lay, a brand-new Remington bolt-action single-shot .22 rifle. He was ecstatic. His mom had played the ultimate parent's prank. Within the hour, a happy young man had grabbed his new cap with earflaps, and a pocketful of biscuits and bacon left from breakfast, and was in the woods.

I now realize the great sacrifice my mom made to buy that rifle. In 1963 there were no outdoor stores or gun shops. Mom had the general store owner order the rifle. Every Friday after work, she would cash her paycheck and then stop by the store and make a payment on my gun. Today, it would seem like a small thing to purchase, as our culture is so affluent. I realized even then, however, that the gift my mom struggled to buy was a big deal. That gun was at my side continually. I never loaned it to anyone. It was my treasure.

Years later I gave the rifle to my brother Steve to keep in the family. After several years, he gave it back, saying I needed to pass it on to my children. When he was old enough, I handed it down to my son. It now belongs to his son, Dakota. The .22 is still in good working order and remains a family heirloom. Today I own six hunting rifles. Most of them reside in the gun cabinet for long periods of time, but when I pick up the Remington .22, my mind goes back to special time. A day

The art of being generous with what you have prepares you for what you may receive in the future.

when giving a gift like that rifle would require great sacrifice. I am not saying I would like to return to that period of time. I would say though that I wish we could go back to that spirit. I appreciate the little things now more than ever. Children often leave gifts for me on my desk at church. Sometimes it's a candy bar or a picture colored for me by a Crayola artist. To enjoy those gifts is to realize their worth. The art of being generous with what you have prepares you for what you may receive in the future. The obscure and unknown have always been a favorite with the Lord. He used a teenage boy with a slingshot to change the course of a war. He used the birth of the Son in an obscure village barnyard to change the world. Small things have a good chance of becoming large things when loosely held. The tighter we attempt to hold on to the small things, the less likely we are to see greater things.

Curtis Howells, a hunting buddy of mine from our church, maintained some acreage that held some really nice deer. He invited me to join him during the hunting season. He worked to insure that we had every opportunity to harvest a nice buck. During the muzzle loader season I shot a large eight point buck. While Curtis did not get a buck, he was excited for me. I have always remembered that generous spirit to give away that which he could have reserved for himself.

If you can enjoy the experience of the hunt or the fishing trip without demanding high expectations of success, you may just become a "small thing" thinker. If the memories you make in the outdoors become as valuable as the gear you use to get there, then there is hope for you. This is Christmas Day 2015. It was fifty-two years ago today that I received my first rifle. Time has nothing to do with the memories I have of that morning. It is in my hard drive of thought.

To embrace the insignificant is a character trait we all need to practice. Christmas can be depressing to many because of all the memories of how things used to be. Our brain is wired to remember. Put everything you can into your memory bank, for there will come a day when that is all you are left with. We are nurturing a culture that believes it is owed an opportunity for success. We are at a bad place when there is no value in the little things of life. If we think we are owed something greater than what we have, we are a part of the problem, not the solution. Small things built this country into the greatest demonstration of liberty the world has ever known.

Don't despise the day of small things. Embrace them. I do not want to be careless with the things the Lord has blessed me with. If they turn into greater things, I will rejoice, but if they continue to be the seed for patience, then I will enjoy that as well.

To my recollection, I never shot anything but a few squirrels with my Remington bolt-action .22 rifle. There are no trophy kills accredited to its power and accuracy. But there is a gentle breeze of memory that still comes over me every Christmas morning; it's the memory of small things.

CHAPTER 20

Full Draw

(The Final Act of Commitment)

Only fear the Lord and serve Him in truth
with all your heart; for consider what
great things He has done for you.
—1 Samuel 12:24

Coming to full draw with your bow is the final step in preparation before letting your arrow fly to its target. It is an exciting moment that has adrenalin pumping through your body. Coming to full draw is the instant when you are totally committed to make the shot but need to wait for something else to happen. Maybe the buck needs to take one more step out of the tree line before firing. Whatever the delay, a full draw hunter is committed to the final act of harvesting an animal.

Before the lightweight compound bows were introduced, I used a Browning Wasp recurve bow. They were hard to string, difficult to bring to full draw, and almost impossible to hold at full draw. Then the 80 percent let-off compound bows revolutionized the sport. A hunter can now commit to full draw with little motion. Even better, full draw can be held until that last piece of the puzzle is in place to complete the shot.

Knowing the exact time to come to full draw is what separates good hunters from great ones. You have to be in that position enough times to know when to make that final commitment. The longer a hunter stays at full draw, the greater the potential for things to go wrong. So it is all about timing. Every good hunter is aware that they are in control of very little. We cannot control the wind or make a buck take that final step for a good shot. At full draw in a ground blind for a wary gobbler may require up to two minutes. Attempting to be up close to a turkey in your blind and make a seven-yard shot to his head means that anything can happen. Remember your twenty hard pin is going to shoot low at five yards. Shooting from a chair inside the blind is just one more thing that makes full draw one tough job.

I love the full draw. In it the hunter becomes the symbol of dedication and commitment. At full draw, the hunter can do nothing but wait for what must happen next. Many times the hunter is forced to release from full draw because the shot never came to the hunter. Good hunters know that sometimes it just does not happen. Bow hunters are used to disappointment. They have to perform with stealth at very close range from their target. Up close, anything can happen.

In 1992 Matt McPherson invented the single-cam technology that revolutionized the bow industry. While competition bows are still about forty inches, the new short bows on the market are fast and light. A young hunter recently saw me with my Matthews bow that is almost sixteen years old. He looked it over and said," Man, that thing is too long." He went on his way and I thought, "No hunter ever came down from their stand after missing a buck and said, 'I would have hit that deer if only my bow was three inches shorter." I take more stock in a hunter that keeps his equipment in working order, and diligently practices shooting from every possible angle. Full draw declares trust in your equipment and confidence in your ability to complete the shot.

To be a devoted follower of Jesus Christ requires us to be fully prepared and totally committed to His will for our lives. Paul makes an impact statement from Romans twelve," And be not conformed to this world: but be transformed by the renewing of your mind, that you may prove what is that good, and acceptable, and perfect will of God." That is commitment.

> *A full draw Christian recognizes that difficult times will always require strong faith and an uncompromising spirit toward the world, the flesh, and the devil.*

To be spiritually alert, is the (full draw) for the Christian. Paul calls that ... fully girded, or totally prepared to take the next step. To wear the whole armor of God as Paul mentions in Ephesians is a believer at full draw. A full draw Christian recognizes that difficult times will always require strong faith and an uncompromising spirit toward the world, the flesh, and the devil. The church needs leadership. Families are desperate for it. The American workplace is falling apart from lack of it. The political system in our country has unraveled without it. Leadership comes from committed people who do the right thing regardless of the cost. Full draw believers are committed to be consistent in their walk with Christ and become great leaders.

Bow hunters are passionate about their sport. They pay close attention to detail. They have a favorite broad head; they are specific about their arrow fletching and its color. They are stealth minded about every part of their gear. That's the kind of believers the church needs today ... believers at full draw.

> Go afield with a good attitude, with respect for the forest and fields in which you walk. Immerse yourself in the outdoor experience. It will cleanse your soul and make you a better person.
> —Fred Bear

CHAPTER 21

Dream Catcher

(Passing on a Dream to the Dreamless)

And they said one to another,
behold, the dreamer comes.
—Genesis 37:19

We have all seen the tourist shop dream catchers. The story behind them is true. "Long ago an old Lakota spiritual leader was on a mountain and had a vision. In his vision Iktomi the great trickster and teacher of wisdom appeared in the form of a spider. The spider took a willow hoop adorned with beads and feathers and began to spin a web. After completing it he said that the web would catch the good dreams and the hole at the center of the web would allow the bad dreams to fall through the web. Traditionally, a Sioux Indian family would hang the dream catcher over the door of their lodge." (Akta Lakota Museum & Cultural Center (aktalakota. stjo.org))

> *God gives children imagination so that they can explore beyond normal boundaries.*

We understand that our destiny cannot be determined by the

hanging dream catcher. Children need to dream. God gives children imagination so that they can explore beyond normal boundaries. It is a proven safe way for a child to soar past reality for an adventure that is limited only by the extent of their imagination. As a child I had more than two hundred acres of woods, fields, and creeks to host my adventures. My mother never heard the words "I'm bored" from me. There was just no time to be bored. My granddad was a dream catcher. Sometimes when the day was done and the supper dishes cleared away I would sit on the front porch with him and tell him of the exploits that had filled my day. He never made fun of them. He nurtured them by simply playing along.

Reading was another way of escaping reality and living a life through the hero of the book. Before the high tech revolution we had radio and three channels of black and white television. Books were the escape for adventure and mystery. I talk to children today and ask what they are reading. While many still read, there is an alarming trend of nonreaders among children. The invention of the mobile device has fast tracked children to an advanced form of games that build hand to eye skills but do little to create imagination or dreaming. This has led to children spending more time connected to Wi-Fi than to the great outdoors.

Hunting and fishing are billion dollar industries. There are outdoor channels and outdoor stores everywhere. The availability to access the outdoor world is there, but the dream of adventure seems lost. While hunting and fishing can be an expensive start up sport, the dream to be in the outdoors is free. The only requirement is for a dream catcher to introduce a child to the possibilities of the outdoors. Camping is inexpensive and a great front door to the imagination of a child. President Theodore Roosevelt provided his five children a campfire in the back yard of the White House. There is no greater magnet to a child than a crackling campfire with the golden embers floating above the warmth. Adults who are willing to invest into a child's life by introducing the outdoors to them become dream catchers. After our son was born my wife, Jan, would place him in his carrier on the floor of the boat, make a shade over him, and we fished. When Shawn was still in diapers he would run after his grandfather so that he could work the trotlines on the Arkansas River. That beginning placed in him a lifelong passion for the outdoors.

Children dream less today because they are consumed with the instant gratification games that mobile devices offer. I am not advocating that these instruments become off limits, as our children are a part of this information highway that rules our existence. They must be able to navigate this world in order to be successful. However, a balance is needed in the mind and heart of a child. The outdoor world will never dominate our way of life in the fast paced lifestyle of our families. They can provide, though, a beautiful perspective of God's creation. Seeing wildlife in their natural environment and making memories of late night campfires with s'mores can relax a child's mind and allow them to dream. It brings us closer to God when we walk through a forest in the fall with the red and orange leaves carpeting our path. To sit at a streams edge with a child and a fishing rod is to escape the lure of the smart phone. To hike along a mountain trail and find a waterfall that has made its music for hundreds of years is God's remedy for a depressed spirit.

Children can dream again, but they need dream catchers. Someone is going to have to shine a light toward the woods. Someone must take the time to explore a stream and bait the hook that just might catch the heart of a child.

If we are to see that hunting and fishing become a reality to today's child we must be the dream catchers for them. If you have ever tried to get a teenager to put their cell phone down you know how great the challenge really is. But if you have ever sat beside a girl or boy as they took their first shot or caught their first fish, you know this dream is possible.

Children today grow up with words like *terrorist, insurgents,* and *ISIS.* They see their mothers and fathers returning home from facing enemies that are endangering their way of life. They live with worry of being the causality of a crazy person desiring to be the object of a television news cast. The greatest gift that we can give our children is the faith to trust God with their lives. To know the love and forgiveness of Jesus Christ will be their greatest security. To give them the dream of experiencing God's great outdoors is not just an opportunity for us; it is our responsibility.

CHAPTER 22

Blue-Sky Speculation

(No Limits Thinking)

Is anything too difficult for the Lord?
—Genesis 18:14

He said to them, "Because of your little faith." For
truly, I say to you, if you have faith like a grain
of mustard seed, you will say to this mountain,
'Move from here to there,' and it will move
and nothing shall be impossible for you."
—Matthew 17:20 (ESV)

Nobody could dream like Walt Disney. He created the entire Disney cosmos with the power of a dream. His thinkers and planners are called "Imagineers." There is a saying among the Imagineers called "Blue Sky Speculation." It simply means that when they get into a room to discuss a matter, the sky is the limit when it comes to thinking. Taking the lid off of our thinking and dreaming gives each of us blue-sky possibilities. We are bound by what we think. If we are told as children we will never be able to do a certain thing, the blue-sky thinking is removed. We live under the law of the lid. Most people never rise above that lid that someone placed over them. You may be thinking, *What in the world does this have to do with hunting or fishing?* The answer is clear. Where do you think all of the blue sky is?

Last summer after conducting our annual leadership camp for youth in Gunnison, Colorado, we enjoyed a few days in Lake City, Colorado. I love to fish in that area. The snow runoff had the streams too high and muddy to do much trout fishing so I made my way down to Dan's Fly Shop to visit with Mr. Dan. For more than fifty years, this man has shown others how to fish and how to enjoy life in a deeper fashion. I have purchased two fly rod combos from Mr. Dan. But to tell you the truth, I stop in his shop each year to hear his stories. They come alive with each telling. This guy loves living. His passion for fly-fishing falls from his lips with no effort. His love for Christ and for others is even a deeper passion.

Mr. Dan took me outside his shop one day. He handed me a fly rod and said, "Let me see what you got." I was so intimidated. Here I am standing with a fishing legend who wants to watch me cast. Before I could strip the fly line off the reel, Mr. Dan looked up to the heavens and said, "Preacher, have you ever seen a more beautiful sky than that?" Mr. Dan is a blue-sky thinker.

We went back into his shop and he invited me back to his workshop where he attempted to teach me two of his secret knots. That exercise ended in dismal failure. I am the worst knot-tying man on the planet. I almost failed my Eagle Scout review because of all those knots. I left Dan's Fly Shop with new flies, and new information of where to cast them. My best purchase though was the encouragement of a blue-sky thinker who reminded me that every day brings an opportunity to take the lid off and dream. My love for the woods and water is not bound by what I might shoot or catch. When under the open blue skies, the lid comes off. Being outdoors allows us to see just how big those possibilities really are. Outdoor people always have a bit of a windblown look. That comes from allowing nature to have its way with us. Whether storm or full sun, we are willing to have chapped lips, dry skin, and red face because we are outdoor blue-sky people.

Jesus sometimes grew weary of people asking the same question over and over. One day a man asked, "Why can't we do what you are doing?" Jesus looked at the beautiful mountain in front of them and said, "If you have faith as a grain of mustard seed you can say to that mountain, move." Matthew 17:20 (KJV) Talking to mountains requires a blue-sky type of thinking. "Hey mountain, get out of my way." That is the jest of how the Lord wants us to think. God wants to bless our faith. Jesus spent a great deal of time outdoors, and we all know He was a master fisherman that loved camping and teaching the disciples around camp fires.

> *Jesus spent a great deal of time outdoors and we all know He was a master fisherman that loved camping and teaching the disciples around camp fires.*

We live in a fallen world, one that desperately needs people of faith to look up again. To see the blue skies of possibility and have faith that God will see us through these troubled times is imperative. Look up, my friends, for our redemption is drawing nigh. If some mountains need moving in your life, begin by taking the lid off of your faith and see how the Lord has been faithful to you. Join the club today: the Blue Sky Thinkers Club.

CHAPTER 23

He Made the Stars Also

(Finding Your Place)

And God made two great lights; the greater
light to rule the day, and the lesser light to
rule the night: He made the stars also.
—Genesis 1:16

lthough this last phrase reads like an afterthought stuck at the end of a sentence, it has great significance. The same God who balances the cosmos with a sun and a moon has no trouble flinging a few stars in the galaxy as well. The sun is just one of the one hundred billion stars in the Milky Way Galaxy, and it is God's greater light. That fact is a wakeup call about the billions of little stars that God has a great eye for detail. Every star is a special creational act of God. While that makes me feel small when compared to the workings of this universe, it reinforces the thought that we matter to Him.

> *The same God who balances the cosmos with a sun and a moon has no trouble flinging a few stars in the galaxy as well.*

Each human matters. Every life has been given breath by God. Every heart that is beating does so by the grace of God.

When I sometimes question my significance in the grand scheme of things, I just look up. While the one hundred billion stars we see are not the sun or the moon, they were still created by God and they shine where they were placed. Every trip to the woods or the water is a reminder that God has created all of this beauty just for us. I seem to have a more thankful spirit upon returning from an outdoor experience. There is a realignment of my soul. It is not due to how successful I was on that trip. Whether or not I caught fish seems to have little to do with that realignment. It seems rather to be connected directly to the experience of being where God's creation is actually absorbed into the body.

Huffington Post did an article about children with ADHD playing and exercising outside in the sun and on green grass. These children showed fewer symptoms than those who played indoors. Sufficient vitamin D is difficult to get through our food and supplement intake. The *Post* went on to say that 80-90 percent of vitamin D should be soaked in through the golden rays of the sun. The *Journal of Aging Health* said, "Getting outside on a daily basis may help older people stay healthy and functioning longer. People in the study showed fewer complaints of aching bones or sleep problems." Other research reveals that gardening can help dementia and stroke patients improve social skills and confidence, while even increasing mobility and dexterity.

Seattle-based environmental psychologist Judith Heerwagon tells the *Huffington Post,* "Just looking at a garden or trees or going for a walk, even if it's in your own neighborhood, reduces stress." She continues. "I don't think anyone understands why, but there's something about being in a natural setting that shows clear evidence of stress reduction, including physiological evidence—like lower heart rate." In 1982 the Japanese Ministry of Agriculture, Forests, and Fisheries even coined a term, *shinrinyoku,* which means taking in the forest, or forest bathing to relieve stress on the body.

I also think that the scents of the outdoors, like the wild flowers and pine, provide a stress-buster effect upon the body. While this is not a medical or science journal, there is so much evidence that points to the outdoors as God's healing remedy for both body and soul. The lion and bear killer David stepped outside once and his reflection of that experience is expressed in chapter 8 of the book of Psalms.

When I consider Your heavens, the work of Your fingers, the moon and the stars, which You have ordained; What is man that You take thought of him, and the son of man that You care for him?

The king was a better man because of soaking up God's natural health spa. He gained a better perspective about himself by spending time under the canopy of the stars. I hate the commercial rhetoric that implies that we get outdoors to lose weight, walk in the park to lose weight, or hike trails to lose weight. That should be the by-product of being outside. Be outdoors to soak your soul. Be in His grand garden to restore peace and balance in your life.

I once moved a staff meeting outside in the sun. I circled the chairs on the parking lot and had coffee with the staff. The first few moments were awkward, but as the light spring breeze and the warm sun energized us, it became natural.

When I camo up and get in my old Chevy pickup, or head to the boat with my fishing rod, there is more going on than just getting away. The great naturalist John Muir wrote, "Climb the mountains and get their glad tidings." Those glad tidings are saying to each of us, "He made the stars also."

CHAPTER 24

The Unspoken Truth

(Why Men Climb Trees and Other Sad Stories)

I can do all things through Christ
which strengthens me.
—Philippians 4:13

It is thirty-four degrees right now, and I am writing this from an outside deck overlooking the Taneycomo River in Hollister, Missouri. My North Face sweater is all that is keeping me from freezing. My wife thinks I am wacky since there is a beautiful fireplace and central heat inside our little rented cabin. Sitting outside this morning actually lends itself to the question of why men still climb trees. Why do we load up fishing gear and head out to a stream when it is thirty-four degrees? These questions are never really discussed by us older outdoorsmen. There is a

> *All the preparation and all of the getting up at 4:30 a.m. instantly paid off. Instant gratification is not part of the outdoors world. Satisfaction seldom ever comes that way.*

secret code among us. We don't talk about the real reason why we do these things.

A few years ago while fishing in a high country beaver pond with a tiny mosquito fly, it was so cold that when I would strip the fly line and retrieve it, the water would freeze in the rod guides between each cast. You really have to want to fish to do that. So back to the question "Why do men climb trees?" Why do we fish when we should probably be sitting by the fire? The answer is not that complicated, but it is a taboo subject among us. We will ramble toward the answer, but there is more research to prove that my hypothesis is correct.

On December 5, 2015, while hunting in Kansas with hunting pal Steve Malone, I was fortunate to kill a trophy Kansas buck at 11:04 a.m. It was overcast and the wind was blowing a cold breeze over the creek. My stand was about seventeen feet high. I shoot left-handed and the buck appeared on my blind side, but I had kept my body turned so that I could shoot from the left hand in an instant. Turns out, an instant was all I had. The giant was chasing a doe but turned to see another doe that was exposed in a clearing about fifty yards from my stand. Everything changed in an instant. All the preparation and all of the getting up at 4:30 a.m. instantly paid off. Instant gratification is not part of the outdoors world. Satisfaction seldom ever comes that way.

The same is true of life. Joy is a process, not instant gratification. Marriage is a long-term partnership that requires patience. Growing your children into responsible, tax-paying, bona fide adults has nothing to do with instant gratification.

I do not hunt so that I can have an adrenaline rush. I do not fight mosquitoes on a hot summer evening while fishing on the Arkansas River to be instantly gratified in the experience. There is a reason, however, and there is a purpose. I know a hunter who has two knee replacements and one hip replaced. He still hunts; he still fishes. He experiences pain when he engages in those activities, yet he still does it. There must be a reason. Well, enough stalling. There is a reason.

We do it because it is the only true test that can determine whether or not we are *still able to do it.*

I told you the answer was simple. When a man reaches the point that he cannot climb into his stand, or keep his balance in a kayak while navigating class 3 whitewater and throwing a Rio Grande fly and nymph rig at the same time, he knows life is about to change.

That change is inevitable. We all understand that it is coming. But as I said, it's a taboo subject. We will not discuss the matter. We simply will know that we must hunt from the ground and fish from the bank. This is not something we are going to have group discussion over; it will just happen. It is an unspoken truth. It just happens. Older men hunt closer to the road and fish a little closer to the dock.

Maybe this unspoken truth can help you to understand why we do what we do. My hands are now frozen. The deck that overlooks the Taneycomo has lost its allurement. The cold Missouri wind has won. The chapter is finished and I am headed inside the cabin where the fireplace provides the instant gratification of warmth.

Now you know why men climb trees.

CHAPTER 25

Fatal Attraction

(The Achilles' Heel)

Be sober, be vigilant; because your adversary
the devil, as a roaring lion, walks about,
seeking whom he may devour.
—1 Peter 5:8

E very superhero had one: an Achilles' heel. That something that is locked away in the closet that jumps out at the most inopportune time to cause even the strongest superhero to fall. Every man faces this battle. Before the high-tech revolution, the secret sins of men came in the form of purchasing sleazy magazines or visiting dark crowded bars in the late hours of the night. Temptation has always been a problem, and that will never change. We are not superheroes, just ordinary men. To be ordinary is to be a member of a big club. To be extraordinary is to be vigilant about your ordinary behavior. We have an adversary who enjoys being in the closet until just the right moment when weakness sets over our souls.

One of the strangest behaviors in the woods comes from a mature bull elk during the rut. The bull will dig a hole in the ground and urinate in it. He will then lie down and rub himself in the mixture. This is repeated many times. While this sounds and smells repulsive to the human, it is a fatal attraction for the cows he is seeking, and can also be fatal for him. The good elk hunter always has his nose in the wind for that particular sickening smell. While this behavior only takes place for short period of time, it can have disastrous results. It takes less than four seconds for a person to lose their temper. Many bad things can happen from those four seconds of fatal attraction. While everyone who sees you lose your temper is either embarrassed or annoyed by those four seconds of outrage, you, on the other hand, feel vindicated or even righteous about it. The bull elk does not think that he stinks when he cruises the mountainside with his urine/fresh-earth scent. He thinks that he is really on his A game. Sort of like the man wearing enough Obsession for Men that you can smell him from fifty feet away.

The ultimate purpose of the bull elk's behavior is to attract as many cows as possible during the short time that he has. This is also the best time for the hunter to get an up-close shot at a real trophy bull. The bull loses all inhibitions during this time. He pays little attention to his surroundings. He is totally obsessed with himself. I think you can draw the analogy on your own. When we think only of ourselves, we become vulnerable to attacks from Satan and his entire bag of tricks. Peter instructed us to be on guard against Satan's subtle assaults.

Moral failure is common among us. Ethical failure is even more rampant. Our thought life creates our action life. When we finally figure out that we will never make it as a superhero, we also come to terms with the fact that we are ordinary. That is why presidents of nations fall morally. No man lives above temptation when it comes to call. We overcome temptation when we realize that we can't on our own. We have an advocate with the Father, and His name is Jesus. I have a friend, Dale Woodard, a long-time Marvel comic book collector, who put this in perspective for me. According to Dale, most superheroes could fly and had a cape. They all lived with a deep hurt and had experienced a difficult past that drove them to act as a superhero. Batman's parents were killed in front of him as a small child. Superman's planet was blown up, Spider-Man's uncle was killed, Captain America had to live outside of his own time line, the Hulk had anger-management issues off the charts, and Iron Man was an alcoholic. They all had issues. They all had to overcome their past. Perhaps the incredible popularity of these superheroes is that every man can identify with the ordinary in these guys.

We must be intentional when dealing with our own Achilles' heel. To give room to today's temptation only makes the next one more difficult to overcome. I love the outdoors. It doesn't matter if I am chopping kindling for our fireplace or standing waist deep with a fly rod in a trout stream. The outdoors forces me to think. It provides an opportunity to delete files that really need to go. Every moment of anger, lust, greed, selfishness, bitterness, and pity can be deleted when we are ready to let it go. It is vital to every man to sweep through the files of his mind

> *It is vital to every man to sweep through the files of his mind so that the new day is not forced to carry yesterday's baggage.*

so that the new day is not forced to carry yesterday's baggage. "Be sober. Be vigilant." 1 Peter 5:8 (KJV) The roar of our adversary makes a big noise. His roar is intimidating. The lion can paralyze his prey just with a roar. There is a fatal attraction in every one of us. Your best self-efforts can never sustain you over the long haul of life. Superman lost his powers when he came into contact with kryptonite. We ordinary guys lose our powers when we forget that the roar of the lion is the perfect time to cowboy up and do the right thing.

CHAPTER 26

GPS

(God's Provision Satisfies)

And my God shall supply all your need according
to His riches in glory by Christ Jesus.
—Philippians 4:19

In 1957 the Russians surprised the world with the launch
of its Sputnik satellite. Scientists from MIT noticed that
the frequency of the radio signals transmitted by the small
Russian satellite increased as it approached and decreased
as it moved away. This was caused by the Doppler Effect,
the same thing that makes the timbre of a car horn change
as the car rushes by. This gave the scientists a grand idea.
Satellites could be tracked from the ground by measuring
the frequency of the radio signals they emitted, and
conversely, the locations of receivers on the ground could
be tracked by their distance from the satellites. That in
the nutshell is the foundation of modern GPS.

-A brief history of GPS by Mark Sullivan,
senior editor of Tech-Live, PCWorld.com.

The US Navy built the first system in 1959. We enjoy this amazing tool today because of the military. It was a Cold War tool of the 1960s that has expanded to thirty-one operational satellites under the authority of the US Air Force.

I purchased my first GPS in 2000. It was not that complicated, but I am not a tech guru so it took a while to get familiar with it. My real challenge was not in marking waypoints; it was trusting the handheld device over my own instincts. I would mark a waypoint at my four-wheeler but also mark my point with pink ribbon or a glow tack just for insurance. I studied the GPS instruction book. I learned all the ins and outs of the little miracle machine. However, I just could not trust it. Finally, one morning I drove my four-wheeler deep into a national forest. I marked my waypoint and left my four-wheeler without marking the trail with ribbon or tacks. While I was scouting for a good place for early fall deer hunting, my primary purpose was to learn to trust my GPS. That day made a believer out of me. When I pulled out my GPS and pulled up the waypoint I had marked earlier that morning, I was much farther out in the woods than I thought. I took off in the direction that the unit pointed out for me. About an hour later, I was at my four-wheeler and headed home fully convinced that I could trust this invention.

For many years, I have relied on my GPS unit to get me in and out of the woods. Once while hunting in the Flattop Wilderness area of Colorado, I used it to mark the spot where I hid my outer hunting coat as the weather turned off hot and I didn't want to pack it any longer. I never doubted for a moment that my handheld GPS would lead me back to the heavy wool jacket.

Fast-forward about fifteen years. While hunting on the Black River in eastern Arkansas with my son, Shawn, and hunting buddy, Matt Brown, I marked Matt's boat as a waypoint on my GPS and we all headed in different directions. I got on a game trail about half a mile from the river and followed it until it opened up nicely into a hardwood flat. I set up a ground blind and hunted there until I lost shooting light. I pulled out my GPS and retrieved the waypoint back to the boat. My trust in the unit was so strong that even while the sun was setting over the wrong shoulder and the river was not flowing in the right direction, I blindly followed the device. What should have been a fifteen-minute walk back to the river had now become a thirty-minute hike in the wrong direction. I took out the batteries and replaced them, but the GPS continued to send me in the same direction. I finally shut it off and pulled out my compass. I made it to the boat with no problem, but my faith had been shaken in the unit that had never failed me.

Upon returning home, I tested again and again the reliability of that device that had pointed me home for so many years. I finally came to the conclusion that the GPS had worn itself out and could never be trusted again. It sits in a drawer today. I cannot make myself part with it, but I can never trust it again. Shopping for a new handheld GPS has started the whole trust issue over again. The new ones have touch screens. They have so many features and maps that I may have to take a course to figure it all out. There is another system of trust in my life, however, that has never failed me. God's Provisional System has been working in my life for more than sixty years. It was put in place upon my salvation as a boy. It is not battery operated and contains much more than maps of the area. It contains the unconditional promises of God.

God has always been faithful. He has always met my needs. There have been moments when my trust of His GPS has faltered. In those moments of weakness, His provision never failed. We all question God from time to time. In the deepest moments of our pain, we cry out, "Why?" I love what C. H. Spurgeon once said. "While we cannot always see the hand of God, we can always trust the heart of God." He meets our needs not based on our goodness but upon the act of His Son, Jesus. Calvary has made this arrangement possible for everyone who calls upon the name of the Lord.

> *Spurgeon once said, "While we cannot always see the hand of God, we can always trust the heart of God."*

CHAPTER 27

The Coming Storm

(The Tide of Public Opinion)

Our government rests in public opinion. Whoever can
change public opinion, can change the government.
—Abraham Lincoln

There was much grumbling among the crowds
concerning Him; some were saying, "He is a
good man," others were saying, "No, on the
contrary, He leads the people astray."
—John 7:12

When Jesus was a boy, He found favor with God and with
man. During His ministry, however, people took sides
for and against Him. At the end of His life, crowds were
screaming for His death. Public opinion had turned. The masses wanted
political change. Jesus was sent to bring spiritual change. He never allowed
the public opinion to deter Him from His mission. Enduring public
humiliation, physical suffering, and eventually death, He asked the Father
to forgive those who had inflicted such horrible treatment. Jesus was a
master at dealing with both religious and political leaders. Truth was the
only weapon that He needed.

Today, there is a public opinion storm coming to this country. Literally every day in the news we are forced to hear another argument about what must be done to stop mass shootings. Every lead story reveals the great danger of terror and what law must be enacted to protect us. The problem is that while the chatter and bantering are nonstop, mass shootings continue and terror is constant. Many lawmakers believe that if they can pass just one more law about gun ownership we will be free of incidents like Ferguson, Missouri, and Baltimore.

As hunters, we own guns. Gun ownership is at an all-time high among American citizens. We threaten no one with them. We keep them locked away when not in use. We teach gun safety above all things to our children. We enjoy freedom here unlike any other country on earth. Those freedoms that we cherish are in danger. Public opinion is largely formed from news organizations that use every angle to convince voters that this is a simple issue of ownership. The notion that if American citizens will just give up their hunting rifles, shotguns, and pistols we will have a secure future is ludicrous. The response from American gun owners to this socialist opinion just creates more headlines for activist journalists to promote their next story of gun violence. I recently was in a large store in town when a man entered wearing camo. He got looks from people that were surprising to me. Their response to him was one of caution. We live in a rural community where it is commonplace for a hunter dressed in camo to stop off at a store for supplies. If public opinion is changing in a state like Arkansas that receives $1.4 billion each year from hunting and fishing, imagine how states like New York and California are changing the minds of their citizens.

This coming storm has been brewing for years. As avid sportsmen and women, our only agenda is preservation. Preserving the woods and waterways handed down to us from our forefathers must be a constant vigil for us. We

> *When children come to accept the philosophy that there are no moral absolutes, the battle will then be lost.*

can no longer just demand that our rights be granted as though our government is doing us a big favor by allowing us to own a gun or to hunt and fish. The battleground is much larger than our rights. This is a battle for the minds and hearts of the next generation. Already our children are taught to think that it is perfectly normal to change your gender or to live in a same-sex civil union. It is not that big of a step to decide that the constitution is no longer necessary to govern us. When children come to accept the philosophy that there are no moral absolutes, the battle will then be lost. This coming storm will not be enacted by an executive order or a vote in Congress but from a coming generation who will have no clear understanding of freedom and the vigilance required to keep it.

Our government can ban guns, knives, sticks, and even rocks, but it will never find a way to ban evil.

CHAPTER 28

The J.C. Penny Hole

(Shopping for Rainbows)

Launch out into the deep and let
down your nets for a catch.
—Luke 5:4

We were in Durango, Colorado, for our annual youth leadership camp. As always, the most difficult part of the trip was just getting all the kids there with their money and belongings and our sanity. Russell White, our city police chief in Alma, has served as chief bus driver for years. He also doubles as a cook and trout stream tester. I had picked up a book in a fly-fishing shop about fishing the waters of southwest Colorado. It was written by a Colorado fisherman and contained some great tips about local waters.

I read a chapter of the book about the Animas River, which flows right through the middle of downtown Durango. The author said that if you are looking for a good place to fish while in Durango, look for the J.C. Penney store. That intrigued me. Directions said to go around behind the store and park in the lot there, look for a path that goes down to the river, and follow it. Sure seemed simple enough. So Chief White, Shawn,

Justin Leonard, an associate pastor, and I all went to the J.C. Penney store to shop for trout.

The book failed to mention the number of long water snakes that inhabited the area. Justin was about twenty yards upstream from me when I heard him scream over the rushing stream. He said, "A snake just came right past me." I screamed back, "I know he came over the top of my Crocs." That was it for Justin, as that snake had to have been over five feet long.

We continued fishing for a while with no positive outcome. The river was running high from snow runoff and we couldn't seem to find any lure or bait that we could keep in the water. Chief noticed that grasshoppers were flying about on the grass-covered hill overlooking the backside of J.C. Penney. Chief caught one and placed it on a hook with a large weight attached to it. He made a cast below a huge boulder that formed a small eddy pool. *Bamm!* The fight was on. Fighting a large rainbow in a moving stream with light tackle presents a real challenge for any angler. Shawn realized that the bait change had struck success and off to the hillside he ran to find another hopper. He rigged up the hopper dropper and found another boulder to pitch it to. Instant success. The river made so much noise that all we could do to communicate was scream and make hand signs. I heard enough to know I was heading to the parking lot hillside to find me a grasshopper. The fish were anxious to have the hoppers, so I became the official grasshopper finder. Have you ever seen three grown men behind a J.C. Penney store on hands and knees catching grasshoppers? We will do what we must in order to catch fish.

I have fished many lakes and streams in Colorado. I love the gold medal waters of the Rio Grande, and I love to fish the Gunnison River, but my most memorable experience in the Mile High state is chasing down grasshoppers in the back of J.C. Penney and flying down the long path to the river to fling a grasshopper below a protruding boulder and waiting for a twenty-inch rainbow to grab it.

There are snakes that sometimes have to be dealt with. While water snakes do not pose a poison problem, any five-foot-long snake that slithers over the top of your footwear can give reason for great concern. I guess you have to decide if the risk is worth the reward. Risk is the price you pay for opportunity. We all take risks daily. It is only when the risk becomes an accident that we realize that there is a price to pay for all risks. I have climbed tree stands for more than thirty years. I always knew there was a risk in climbing them, but it never became an issue until a Missouri fall in 2013. After that fall, I became a harness safety freak. I paid the price, and the risk was not worth the prize. The same is true with sin. We are tempted to do things that we know are wrong. That is sin. Yet we think we can beat the odds. "Be sure your sin will find you out." Numbers 32:23 (KJV) There is no escaping the fact that if we continue in sin, we will be caught. I have never heard anyone caught in their sin say that it was worth the risk.

Sometimes you just have to try things that go against all logic.

There is another lesson in the grasshopper story. Sometimes you just have to try things that go against all logic. To read a book about fishing behind the Durango, Colorado, J.C. Penney store just made no sense, but by faith we gave it a try. Our faith was as small as a mustard seed, but that's about all that God needs to see in order to honor it. Most of my faith life has been on the mustard seed level. Mountains move, however, from that kind of faith. Obstacles vanish from mustard seed faith. It is the small things in life that make giant things happen. Faith is never measured by yesterday's success. It is not sold by the pound. It is far too precious a commodity to weigh out like that. Faith comes in small portions. So small in fact that it almost is unseen by the naked eye.

Peter had fished all night long. He was used to that. He was also accustomed to failure as a fisherman. But when Jesus called to him from the shore, "Hey, Pete, you catching anything?" A new bait was about to be introduced. The *faith* bait. Jesus instructed Peter to move the nets to the other side of the boat. Boy, did Jesus get an earful on that request. "All night long we have toiled at this. I am tired, but nevertheless, at Your word, I will let down a net." Luke 5:5 (KJV) The attitude of the fisherman was not good.

Fishermen can get a little cranky when they go without sleep. They can also get stubborn about new fishing tactics. Faith made the difference. Peter could not think of one time that Jesus had ever lied to him. There was no history of failure when it came to the integrity of the word of Jesus.

We are in the same boat with Peter. We are often weary from life. We are frustrated by our failures. When challenged, we become defensive and hold tightly to our old ways. Life can be expensive when we refuse to implement faith into our daily walk. Peter finally gave faith a try. He had to call for help from the other boats as he dropped his net to the other side of the boat.

We are called to live a life of faith. Our salvation comes to us through faith. The blessings of God come to us through faith. We risk little when we trust the Word of God. He has never failed us and will always meet our need. We may question why He allows things to happen. Bad things happen to good people, and sometimes the worst things happen to the best people, but His grace is always sufficient. His mercy is unfailing. Every time that we trust the Lord, we are creating an opportunity for God to work in our lives.

CHAPTER 29

Corks and Cane Poles

(Building a Life Together)

Therefore shall a man leave his father
and his mother, and shall cleave unto his
wife: and they shall be one flesh.
—Genesis 2:24

My wife, Jan, is the best fishing buddy a man could have. When we were teenagers, I would borrow her dad's pickup, his flat-bottom boat, along with his daughter, and head to the fishin' hole. Jan would pack us a picnic basket and we would explore the lakes, creeks, and ponds. Jan actually knew more about fishing than I did, as her father was a commercial fisherman when she was growing up. She was raised along the Arkansas River near Paris, Arkansas. Going fishing became our primary dating destination. We have always shared a love for the outdoors with our children and grandchildren.

One spring morning, we were crappie fishing in the Arkansas River. We had started dunking minnows before the sun had made its daily appearance. Not having much luck, we took a long boat ride up the river to try small creek not well known. I put the trolling motor down and got the rods out ready to see some bobber bouncing from hungry crappie.

While trolling out of the river into the mouth of the creek, I asked Jan if she was ready for a sandwich. She handed my bologna and cheese sandwich, a bag of chips, and a Coke to me. We have always loved picnics, and nothing is better than a good bologna sandwich. I was running the trolling motor with my foot, holding my sandwich in my left hand and my rod in my right hand. I swiveled my deck seat around to say something to Jan when it happened. The weld on my seat broke from the casting deck. She watched me as in almost slow motion I did a flip, chair and all, into the Arkansas River. When I surfaced, my sandwich, Coke, fly rod, and chair were all headed to the bottom of the river. I had never heard my wife laugh like that before. The trolling motor was locked on the high position causing my shirt to be twisted up in the prop. Now I am fighting the trolling motor while attempting to jump back in the boat. My wife was of little help, as she was still in the floor laughing. She finally stopped laughing long enough to help me get back into the boat. We never caught another fish, but we have shared that memory for many years.

Jan's favorite method of fishing is a long cane pole with a big red and white bobber. She has caught many crappies over the years with her beach-ball-size corks. We have fished through our entire lives together. We began taking our firstborn fishing by locking his car seat onto the floor and building a shade for him to sleep while we fished. Jan and I have talked through our challenges in life with fishing rods in our hands. Communicating with each other while enjoying the outdoors has been a winning combination for us.

Marriages need hope. Hope is the fuel that makes a difference in every relationship. When we talk to each other, hope must be shared. There is so much discouragement in our culture. Husbands and wives have to find a way that keeps hope afloat in these challenging times. Your marriage may not use fishing to keep the lines of communication open, but you can find one thing that shuts the world out while you

> *Hope is the fuel that makes a difference in every relationship.*

reconnect to love and laughter, while learning what your partner needs to hear from you.

Jan baits her own hook. Whether it's a worm for a rainbow trout or a minnow for a spring crappie, she handles her own business. She has her own tackle box and does not share its contents because she says I lose her stuff. In the tough issues of life, we have to be able to bait our own hook. Life can get messy. It can sometimes crush us with the stress that hounds us. Best remedy for me is a fishin' trip with my buddy. She will always have a picnic lunch for us and will certainly find a way to laugh at something that always happens to us while we are on the water. When Jan and I go fishing, it becomes a stress-reducing exercise with corks and cane poles.

> If you want to go fast, go alone. If you
> want to go far, go together.
> —African proverb

CHAPTER 30

Pocketknives and Promises

(Waiting on Tomorrow)

Cause me to hear Your loving kindness in the morning,
for in You do I trust; Cause me to know the way in
which I should walk, for I lift up my soul to You.
—Psalm 143:8

A church friend asked me this week how many pocketknives I have given away. Thinking for a moment, I said, "No idea, but the bigger question may be how many have been given to me?" I have a thing for pocketknives. Even as a boy, I coveted them. My granddad would let me carry his as we made our daily rounds of milking the Jersey cow and feeding the chickens and hogs. To carry his knife made me feel important.

I do enjoy giving knives to people. Sometimes to say thank-you and often to show appreciation for a job well done. While men today have less need to carry a knife, it is still a symbol of our roots. In the past, men carried knives because they knew they would need them. Carrying a knife today is more symbolic than practical, but I have one in my pocket every day. My favorite knife job as a boy was cutting off a piece of twist tobacco for my granddad to chew. My second favorite knife job was to haul a few bales of hay out to the pasture and cut the baling twine with my knife. Having that knife was my way of being prepared for the unexpected.

A few years ago, I was standing in the pre-op room of a Little Rock hospital with David and Julie Wright, a family in our church who were fighting cancer. Every family who has faced this challenge understands the stress this family was experiencing. David was about to go into surgery that would change his life forever. He realized that the surgery was not the end but the beginning of a long journey of treatments that would test every ounce of his resolve.

After we prayed, I walked with Julie beside David's gurney down the long corridor that ended with a set of double doors. The attendant left us a moment outside those closed doors. I reached in my pocket and pulled out my favorite trapper knife that I carried. I put it in David's hand and told him that knife was my promise to him that when he beat this thing, we would plan an elk-hunting trip to Colorado to celebrate. He gave Julie the knife to hold for him as he went to surgery.

While it took lots of healing, and months of treatments, David was able to defeat that cancer. Making life-changing adjustments is never easy. Physical pain and emotional distress are the reminders of cancer's toll on a family.

The hunting trip became a reality the following year. Our road trip with mules, horses, and tents took us to Chama, New Mexico. After a hearty breakfast there, we fed and watered the stock and crossed into Colorado. We got to the Chromo General Store to purchase ice and other things we needed. Before we went into the little store, I told David that the man who ran it was the most unfriendly, grumpy, and foul-mouthed man I had ever known. He would cuss at hunters if he had to fill out a hunting license for them. I hated to go in his store, but it was thirty miles to the nearest town. Well, the next thing I know, David goes in like he owns the store. The owner swears a blue streak at David, asking him, "What the#%#+* do you want?" He asked David why he drove eight hundred miles to hunt in Colorado. David told the old man that he had beaten cancer and was gonna enjoy a hunting trip with his friends. The old grump eased up on his language and actually spoke a kind word to David. My son and I looked at each other in unbelief. David's spirit had now conquered a miserable hard heart. For the rest of our trip, we sent David to deal with the old-timer.

We made our camp at about eight thousand feet above the Navaho River, in the San Juan Mountain range. The state was experiencing drought conditions. We hunted the higher twin peaks but found no elk. The weather was hot and dry, which made the hunt even more difficult. While we were not fortunate to harvest an elk on that trip, it was still a great success. The evening meals around the campfire provided many memories. David soaked up the experience with joy.

Our attitude about what happens to us frames the way that we will deal with life when it crushes us.

My promise to David was to have an adventure together to celebrate his victory over cancer. Those days we spent together served as a reminder to me that there are many things in our lives that we cannot control. Our attitude about what happens to us frames the way that we will deal with life when it crushes us. David has moved forward in his life. He and Julie have two children and serve the Lord faithfully. He has also found a way to encourage others who go through suffering, he still has the trapper pocketknife, and I still love to give knives away.

CHAPTER 31

Like Father, Like Son

(Passing It On)
By Shawn Shelton

The Father loves the Son and has
given all things into His hand.
—John 3:35 (ESV)

There's just something magical about watching the sunrise. I've been blessed to experience many of those moments while listening to the bugle of an elk, riding in a boat headed to my favorite fishing hole, or sitting in a tree while waiting on a big buck.

One of those special moments came while watching the sun fight through a foggy sky on Lake Toho in Florida. The rest of the family was enjoying a day at Disney World while my dad and I were with a local guide, fishing big shiners for

> *The Lord has given us a certain number of sunrises to enjoy. Only He knows how many we have, but I feel it's our duty to make the most of each one we receive.*

some largemouth bass. The morning was quiet; the water was a brilliant blue as I watched my cork go under and the fight was on. I landed a nice eight-pound bass, which was the first of many to come on this incredible day of fishing. My dad and I were both catching bass nearly every cast. We caught several bass in the three- to five-pound range and were having a blast. Then it happened. Dad set his hook on a bass. We immediately knew it was a trophy. The guide was as excited as we were. He grabbed the net while dad was battling the larger-than-life bass. For a while, I wasn't sure who would win the battle. He finally wore the fish down and got it to the boat. The guide, using the net he had found, landed the fish with smiles all around. The giant weighed in at eleven pounds and four ounces. It was the biggest bass Dad had ever caught. I already had an eight-pounder and thought I would have the big one for the day. I was so glad Dad got the bigger one, making it the best day of fishing for both of us. We had used six-dozen shiners by lunch, leaving us without any bait and a morning we will never forget. Fifty-five bass were caught that magical morning, creating a memory neither of us will forget. I can still see that eleven-pounder swimming off, thanking us for letting him return to the grass beds in his home.

This experience reminded me that the Lord has given us a certain number of sunrises to enjoy. Only He knows how many we have, but I feel it's our duty to make the most of each one we receive.

Whether you're enjoying God's creation or sitting in your easy chair, take time to go to God in prayer, thanking Him for your blessings and opportunities that come your way. I remember as a young boy Dad letting a big bass go, and as he was swimming across the top of the water, Dad said he was thanking us for letting him go. I think we, as God's children, are like that bass: we need to thank Him for letting us go.

Shawn's catch of the day

Bob with his Florida bass

Shawn (on right) with his fireman buddy Justin on a pheasant hunt

CHAPTER 32

Who Am I?

(Finding Our Place in Him)
By Steven Malone

When I consider Your heavens, the work of your
fingers, the moon and the stars, which You have
ordained, what is man that you are mindful of him,
and the son of man that you visit him? For You have
made him a little lower than the Angels, and You
have crowned him with glory and honor. You have
made him to have dominion over the works of Your
hands; You have put all things under his feet.
—Psalm 8:3–6

There are two certainties that occur every day in nature: the sun will rise, providing the daylight, and it will set, giving us the night. Every clock in the world is set to this daily miracle from God. These two events give each of us opportunity to enjoy what the Lord has provided every day of our lives. This miracle became a reality one night while standing in a hay field north of the Platt River in the Sand Hills area of Nebraska. It was a beautiful October evening and the Big Dipper was so close that I could almost use it to scoop up a drink of water from the river.

Gazing up at the heavens, I could see the Milky Way, Orion, and Scorpios. There were more constellations, but I could not locate or name them.

That experience took my mind back to think of young David, the future king of Israel, lying in the fields while gazing at the same stars in his father's field and saying, "Who am I?"

On another hunt, I was sitting in a tree stand in north-central Kansas well before dawn. The sting of the frozen air was almost unbearable. The tree I was sitting in was frozen, making it almost impossible to attach my bow holder into the wood. A four-degree morning was challenging this Arkansas hunter's resolve. When the sun began to break over the Conservation Reserve Program field to the southwest of my stand, it looked like a winter wonderland. A heavy frost appeared with the morning light covering the grass. Ice crystals were floating in the frozen air as darkness surrendered. About thirty minutes after daybreak, a doe came running out of the draw to the southeast of my stand, followed closely by a mature eight-point buck. They both entered the large field in front of me. It was like watching a quarter horse working cattle as they played the catch-me-if-you-can game. It was beautiful to see the animals as they kicked up the frost with every step. The ice crystals made the scene almost magical. With each breath, the deer seemed to exhale white smoke upon the wind. Again, I think, *Who am I to get to see His work in creation and witness His beauty?*

That November morning is permanently sealed in my mind.

Another adventure led me high into the British Columbia Rocky Mountains. We rode four-wheelers for six hours deep into the wilderness. After another day and a half, we reached an altitude of eight thousand feet, where we made our base camp. We continued to climb and descend from eight to ten thousand feet, searching for a mountain goat that would score forty-eight inches or better. My guide, Brad, and I spotted several billies, and one of them needed a closer look. Brad made the call that this was our goat to harvest.

After making our approach, we set up above the billy and waited for the perfect opportunity. My heart was pounding as I came to full draw. I released my arrow from twenty-two yards and hit the goat right behind the right shoulder. He ran right toward the cliff, and I just knew he was going to topple right off the two-hundred-foot drop. He disappeared out of sight. We found the trophy about forty yards from the cliff's edge.

After taking photos and reliving the hunt, we quartered up the goat and loaded the meat in our packs. We were facing a three-hour hike back to our base camp, and one

> *My heart was pounding as I came to full draw. I released my arrow from twenty-two yards and hit the goat right behind the right shoulder.*

of those hours would be in total darkness. As the sun began to sink behind the Rocky Mountains, it was a moment to pause and soak in one last look at God's handiwork. Normally, I would be taking pictures, but instead, I just sat and again thought, *Who am I to get to experience such a thing?* This was the most difficult hunt of my life. Fifteen days without a shower, and hiking more miles than I can remember, made this adventure unforgettable. Our society places more value on material things than spiritual. Our private agendas and special interest groups like the animal rights activists cause us to be distracted from the greatest gifts that God provides to us. We have built buildings, bridges, and stadiums, but in all our building, we have never made anything like God's creation, and it's free for us to enjoy.

God sent His Son to save us from our sins. He rose from the grave to seal that promise. When we accept that great gift of redemption by faith, we receive the only thing in life that cannot be taken away. It's the only thing that has eternal value. Who am I to receive such a gift?

> I beseech you therefore, brethren, by the mercies of God,
>   that you present your bodies a living sacrifice, holy,

acceptable into God, which is your reasonable service. And be not conformed to this world, but be transformed by the renewing of your mind, that you may prove what is that good, and acceptable and perfect will of God.

—Romans 12:1–2

Steve with his trophy

Steve's mountain goat hunt

CHAPTER 33

Hearing the Call

By Richard Craft

As the long chill of winter finally gives way to spring, I, much like a six-year-old anticipating Christmas, get so excited in the days leading up to opening day of turkey season. The weeks before the first hunt are filled with scouting birds, bringing the old turkey vest out from storage, practicing on the slate and box call, giving the Remington 11-87 a good cleaning, and making sure everything is ready for the big day.

There is one particular opening day I will never forget. It was the spring of 2004 in Eagle Rock, Missouri. I had invited my pastor, Bob Shelton, to go to the woods with me and my turkey-hunting buddy, Jeff Fletcher. It's an opening morning tradition to get up at 5:00 a.m. and prepare fried, over-easy eggs, crisp, hickory-smoked bacon, biscuits and gravy, coffee, and orange juice. Like a kid on Christmas morning, getting up at 5:00 a.m. is never a problem on the first day of turkey season. Usually, I toss and turn all night while thinking about what the new season will bring and the memories that will be made.

After a great breakfast, the three of us jumped in the truck and drove to the farm where we were planning to hunt. We unloaded all of our gear and crossed through the three-strand barbed wire fence into the open pasture. After about five minutes of walking across the open pasture, we made our way to the top of three benches that led down into a creek bottom. I like to get to a vantage point where I can listen for the first gobble of the morning. Then I can move and get set up depending on where I think the toms have roosted. It's always better to be early than late in order to be able to move in the dark undetected, get to the listening spot, and be ready to move as the woods come alive on a spring morning.

If you have never listened to the woods before sunrise, there is a hierarchy of nature as to how the woods come alive. First, you will hear a few songbirds begin to sing a note or two, followed by the call of the whippoorwills that begin their day with "Whippoorwill, whippoorwill." They are soon joined by the hoot owls, who sing their own song of "Who cooks for you? Who cooks for you?" About this time, you will hear the first gobble of a tom turkey on the roost. It's his way of letting everyone in the woods know that he is awake and ready for the day to begin, especially the hens. It's as if he's telling the ladies, "Here I am, and you need to come see me."

That first gobble will often trigger a chain reaction of gobbles from other toms in the same set of woods. The crows like to get in on the action as well, as they think it is their job to awaken the other woodland creatures with their incessant *caw, caw, caw* sound. The toms are gobbling at everything by now, and the hens are echoing back to the toms with love words of soft, tree yelps sounding like *yelp, yelp yelp yelp, yep*. Just listening to the sound of good gobbling is music to the ears of a turkey hunter. Before the sun ever rises, it's already been a great day. If you are going to move locations, it's best do so under the dimly lit morning light. At this point, it's time to set up and let the hunt begin.

I compare turkey hunting to playing a game of cards. The turkey is the dealer and the hunter must play his best with the hand that he is dealt. The hunter must make the right move in order to increase his chances of winning the hand: bringing the ole tom home in the back of his truck. There are just a few minutes of time to do all this, as the sun is quickly rising. It is important to exercise caution when moving about, in order to not be seen by the turkeys or push them off their roosts. It is also important to remember that turkeys don't wear a watch or watch a clock. They operate on turkey time, and a good turkey hunter must have great patience.

I still remember this morning like it was yesterday. The weather was nice and cool and the cloud coverage was sparse. As the sun began to rise, the wind began to blow. From our vantage point at the top, the wind was blowing so loudly we couldn't hear what was going on down in the creek bottom. The three of us stood there for several minutes, hoping to hear a gobble, but there were none. I knew the turkeys were in the bottom, but not exactly sure where. As the sun began to rise, we knew we had to make our move and get into the edge of the timber without being seen.

I told Bob and Jeff we needed to head toward the creek bottom, find a place to set up, and just see what would happen. That's one of the things about turkey hunting: no two hunts ever seem to be the same. We made it to second bench and I hit my box call. Immediately, we heard several gobbles. I knew, for sure, there were two birds. Maybe even three. I could tell by their gobbles they were across the creek bottom to the south. We then moved to the top of the bottom bench. Bob and Jeff settled in under some cedars, and I found a cedar that gave me good coverage, where I could see the creek bottom. I hit the box call again and heard three separate gobbles. The game was on. We had both played our first card. It was now time to see how the game played out.

I switched over to my slate pot call and gave a few yelps. The turkeys responded with multiple gobbles. I could tell they were closing the distance. It was only a matter minutes and I could see the three amigos on the other side of the creek. They were gobbling and strutting and putting on quite the show, in hopes that the hen doing all the yelping on the ridge would come down to see them. After several minutes of calling with the pot call and watching them strut and gobble, it appeared they were not going to cross the creek. We were set up in a place we could not move, so we had to wait it out. I laid off the call for ten minutes or so and let the gobblers settle down and start feeding in the pasture along the creek. Then I decided it was time to make it or break it and I got on the pot call with some very aggressive cutting and yelping. Two of the gobblers heard the call, pitched across the creek, and were heading up to the ridge where we were settled in the cedar trees. My heart was racing. I thought, *We didn't rehearse what we would do if multiple birds came in.* I was hoping Bob and Jeff were able to see each other and would know when to shoot at the same time.

I continued to purr on the slate and the two amigos gobbled their heads off all the way up the hill. It seemed like it took forever for them to top the hill and come into shotgun range. The gobblers finally crested the hill in full strut, intently looking for the hen. I gave one last soft purr and they both went into double and triple gobbles. As soon as they quit, I heard the roar of the two twelve gauges and saw two gobblers flopping on the top of the ridge. Harvesting one bird is an amazing hunt, but to double up is a thrill of a lifetime that is not often shared. Bob, Jeff, and I were on our feet and running toward the birds in total excitement.

> *It's an awesome feeling walking back to the truck with a gobbler over your shoulder, but to have two riding home in the back of the truck with you is something one won't ever forget.*

Jeff is a former professional fisherman on the Bass Master's tour and qualified for the Bass Master's classic on numerous occasions. He holds the Arkansas state record for striper, yet he never seems to get this excited when he is catching fish. Turkey hunting, however, brings out a whole new level of excitement. This kind of excitement can only happen on a day like the one described. Jeff turned and said a few things in excitement that I will have to keep between the three of us hunting. I was rolling in laughter at his humorous expression, to which he did apologize to the preacher for his words. Bob later said, "The boy sure gets excited." We exchanged a few high fives and gathered our gear.

We tagged our birds and headed back to the truck. All of us were giddy again like the six-year-old on Christmas morning. It's an awesome feeling walking back to the truck with a gobbler over your shoulder, but to have two riding home in the back of the truck with you is something one won't ever forget. To do something you love with two of your best friends is a special blessing from heaven.

This special day all began with our heavenly Father allowing us the time and health to go outdoors and enjoy His creation. Never take for granted the blessing of being out in the woods. Even on a slow day in the woods, you can still see his handiwork when you look around.

This opening day double all began with a few notes on the box call as the gobblers heard the call. My question for you today is "Have you heard a call from our heavenly Father?" What is your response to His voice? Just as the gobblers responded to the call, have you responded to God's call?

The Bible says in John 10:27 (KJV), "My sheep hear my voice and I know them and they follow me." Make sure you hear the voice of God when He is calling you, and respond. I remember a hymn taught to me as a young boy, and the words are still true today.

Jesus Is Tenderly Calling

By Frances J. Crosby (1883)

Jesus is tenderly calling you home—calling today calling today.
Why from the sunshine of love will you roam?
Farther and farther away?
Refrain: Calling today, calling today,
Jesus is calling, is tenderly calling today.

Jesus is calling the weary to rest, calling today, calling today,
Bring him your burden and you shall be
blest; He will not turn you away.

Jesus is waiting, oh come to him now, waiting today, waiting today,

Come with your sins, at his feet lowly bow;
Come, and no longer delay.

Jesus is pleading, oh list to his voice, Hear him today, hear him today,
They who believe on his name shall rejoice;
Quickly arise and away.

Calling today, Calling today,
Jesus is tenderly calling today.

For Whosoever calls upon the Lord shall be saved.
—Romans 10:13 (KJV)

Merriam, Rio Grande, Eastern, Osceola, 2005
2005-All four in the same year-Grand Slam

CHAPTER 34

Hank's Helping Hands

(Paying It Forward)

Let each of you look not only to his own
interests, but also to the interest of others.
—Philippians 2:4 (ESV)

He was a quiet, almost invisible force who always sat on the back row, right corner of the church. When he shook hands with you, you felt like a child because of his giant bearlike paw. He loved his job and was always helping fellow workers down on their luck. Hank never complained about anything or anyone. I do not think that I ever heard him say a negative thing about anyone. His time was short here on earth by our thinking. Life is fragile. We are not in charge of its beginning or its end, but we are in charge of how we live it. Hank lived his life with integrity and character. He never married and left this earth on May 31, 2012, at the age of thirty-four. Hank was a professional welder and a farmer with his dad, Rennie.

> *We are not in charge of its beginning or its end, but we are in charge of how we live it.*

Hank loved to duck hunt and fish. His love for the outdoors, his family, job, and the Lord occupied his time. Hank loved to give. Not just his tithe at church, but his life was one of quietly helping others. He never sought credit or exposure for his good deeds. With Hank, doing right was a reward in itself. Our church was purchasing water filters to take on our next journey to Africa. The filters cost about seventy dollars each. To demonstrate how effective they were, our staff dumped dirt, worms, trash, and other things that I was never sure of into a large glass tank. Then I drank from the ugly mess using the filter. We were asking each family to purchase just one filter. Hank bought ten of them. He was never concerned about having earthly things himself. Hank was a big man who had an even larger heart.

After Hank's death, Shawn met with some of our men about creating a ministry that allowed boys and girls an opportunity to experience the outdoors. Hank's Helping Hands was born. Since then, Hank's crew has taken boys and girls on fishing trips, given scholarships to deserving seniors, and provided deer and turkey hunts to Oklahoma and Kansas. There are many projects in the works for the future.

Every outdoorsman has a responsibility to pay their heritage forward. While I love to catch fish and harvest a deer or turkey, it brings just as much joy to me to watch the eyes of a child when a hunting or fishing trip becomes a reality for them. Investing in the future men and women of this country may just be your greatest legacy. Hank would be proud to see the boys and girls load up in our vans and pickup trucks before heading out to another adventure. I wish that I could understand why things happen. I wish that I could answer all of the whys that plague us from this side of heaven. I realize that no one can provide those answers. The only thing we can do is live every day with purpose and passion.

Outdoorsmen across the United States and around the world form one of the most generous and philanthropic groups that I know. The pay-it-forward mentality of outdoorsmen and women is encouraging. While the halls of Congress debate gun control and Second Amendment rights, the rest of us continue to work, pay taxes, help those in need, and protect this nation's heritage. I would never trust a politician who could not land a fish, shoot a rifle, or put a hole in a ten-ring target. I could never in good conscience elect anyone to any office who did not enjoy backpacking a mountain trail or wading across a stream just to explore the next bend of the river. I have learned more about life while sitting in a duck blind and laughing at life with friends and family than I ever did in any graduate course that I ever took. We have turned this country and its leadership over to weak-knee, politically correct activists who never saw life from the back of a horse or told stories around a campfire after a day's hunt. Our way of life must now be demonstrated to the boys and girls who still have an open mind about the great outdoors and the God who created it all.

We do not worship the outdoors. We do worship, though, the God who created this universe and gave us guardianship over it. Sportsmen make it possible for wildlife habitat to flourish all over this nation. While the animal rights groups beg for money constantly on television, sportsmen take responsibility for the woods and waters with great pride. Our greatest challenge, however, is to pay it forward to the next generation of leaders.

Hank's Helping Hands and hundreds of other such benevolent outdoor programs will help to point boys and girls to the outdoors and to the Lord who gives us such wonderful opportunities. If you would like to be a Hank's Helping Hands crew member, just contact us. On your next fishing or hunting trip, consider taking a boy or girl along. Pay it forward. Hank would be proud if you did.

The only reason I ever played golf in the first place
was so I could afford to hunt and fish.
—Sam Snead

Hank and his mother Alicia

Hank duck hunting

Hank setting Decoys

Hank on a fishing trip with kids

Hank and parents, Alicia and Renny, fishing in Alaska

Hank with his buck

Hank with his ducks

Hank's Helping Hand's Kansas doe hunt

Printed in the United States
By Bookmasters